Joy and Enthusiasm

D1421616

Also by Norman Vincent Peale
and available from
Mandarin Paperbacks

The Power of Positive Thinking
The Power of Positive Living
The Amazing Results of Positive Thinking
Enthusiasm Makes the Difference
A Guide to Confident Living
Inspiring Messages for Daily Living
The Joy of Positive Living
The Positive Principle Today
Positive Thoughts for the Day
The Positive Way to Change Your Life
Power of the Plus Factor
The Power of Positive Thinking for Young People
Stay Alive All Your Life
The Tough Minded Optimist
The New Art of Living
Courage and Confidence

With Kenneth Blanchard
The Power of Ethical Management
(You Don't Have to Cheat to Win)

With Smiley Blanton
The Art of Real Happiness

Also edited by Norman Vincent Peale
Unlock Your Faith-Power

Norman Vincent Peale's
Joy and Enthusiasm

AN ANTHOLOGY EDITED BY

NORMAN VINCENT PEALE

CEDAR

A Mandarin Paperback
JOY AND ENTHUSIASM – AN ANTHOLOGY

First published in Great Britain 1984
by Unwin Paperbacks
This edition published 1990
by Cedar
an imprint of Reed Consumer Books Ltd
Michelin House, 81 Fulham Road, London SW3 6RB
and Auckland, Melbourne, Singapore and Toronto

Reissued 1993

First published in the USA as a Giniger Book, published in
association with Fleming H. Revell Company, Old Tappan, New
Jersey 07675, under the title *Treasury of Joy and Enthusiasm.*

Copyright © 1981 Norman Vincent Peale

A CIP catalogue record for this title
is available from the British Library

ISBN 0 7493 0716 1

Printed and bound in Great Britain
by Cox & Wyman Ltd, Reading, Berks

This book is sold subject to the condition
that it shall not, by way of trade or otherwise,
be lent, resold, hired out, or otherwise circulated
without the publisher's prior consent in any form
of binding or cover other than that in which
it is published and without a similar condition
including this condition being imposed
on the subsequent purchaser.

Acknowledgments

Grateful acknowledgment is made to the following authors, agents, publishers, and other copyright holders for the use of the material quoted in this book. Every effort has been made to locate copyright holders and, if any material has been used without proper permission, the editor would appreciate being notified so that proper credit can be given in future editions.

ABINGDON PRESS, for material from *A Feast for a Time of Fasting* by Louis Cassels and for material from *Abundant Living* by E. Stanley Jones.

STANLEY ARNOLD, for his quotation, "Every problem contains within itself the seeds of its own solution."

FRED BAUER, for his poem "for quiet I like unspeaking trees," from his book *For Rainy Mondays and Other Dry Spells* (Prometheus Press).

ERNEST BENN LTD., for world rights outside the United States and its dependencies and Canada to use excerpts from "The Spell of the Yukon" and "The Three Voices" from *Songs of a Sourdough* by Robert W. Service.

BRANDT & BRANDT LITERARY AGENTS, INC., for material from *Our Town* by Thornton Wilder. Copyright © 1938, 1957 by Thornton Wilder.

BRUCE F. CLIFFE, for material from *Let Go and Let God* by Albert E. Cliffe, copyright © renewed 1979 by Albert E. Cliffe.

COLLLINS PUBLISHERS, for material from the book *More Prayers for the Plain Man* by William Barclay.

CONTEMPORARY BOOKS, INC., for the poem "It Couldn't Be Done" by Edgar A. Guest. Reprinted from *Collected Verse of Edgar A. Guest*, © 1934 with the permission of Contemporary Books, Inc., Chicago.

V.A.P. CRONIN AND READER'S DIGEST for permission to reprint A. J. Cronin's article "The Turning Point in My Career."

DR. DONALD CURTIS, for his affirmation beginning, "I move serenely forward. . . ."

RALPH S. CUSHMAN, for his poem "The Secret" from his book *Spiritual Hilltops*.

DEVORSS & COMPANY, for material from *You Try It* by Robert A.

Russell. Published by DeVorss & Company, Marina del Rey, California.

DODD, MEAD & COMPANY, for excerpts from "The Spell of the Yukon" and "The Three Voices" by Robert Service. Reprinted by permission of Dodd, Mead & Company, Inc. from *The Collected Poems of Robert Service*. Copyright 1907, 1909, 1912, 1916, 1921 by Dodd, Mead & Company, Inc. Copyright 1940 by Robert W. Service.

DOUBLEDAY & COMPANY, INC., for "In the Garden of the Lord" by Helen Keller, from *Masterpieces of Religious Verse*, edited by Charles L. Wallis, copyright 1948 by Harper and Brothers; excerpt from *Only in Alaska* by Tay Thomas, copyright © 1969 by Mary P. Thomas; excerpt from *Great Possessions* by David Grayson, copyright 1917 by Ray Stannard Baker; excerpt from *The Greatest Book Ever Written* by Fulton Oursler, copyright 1951 by Fulton Oursler; for material by Arnold Bennett. All selections reprinted by permission of Doubleday & Company, Inc.

WILLIAM B. EERDMANS PUBLISHING COMPANY, for excerpt from *C. S. Lewis—Images of His World* by Douglas Gilbert and Clyde S. Kilby.

EVANGELICAL PUBLISHERS, for the poem "What God Hath Promised" by Annie Johnson Flint.

GUIDEPOSTS MAGAZINE, for material from "Fragile Moments" by Phyllis I. Martin. Copyright 1973 by Guideposts Associates, Inc. Used by permission from *Guideposts Magazine*.

HARPER & ROW PUBLISHERS, INC., for "Joy," pp. 77-78 in *A Gift for God* by Mother Teresa, copyright © 1975 by Mother Teresa Missionaries of Charity; for specified excerpts from *On Happiness* by Pierre Teilhard de Chardin, English translation copyright © 1973 by Wm. Collins Sons Ltd; for "I Shall Be Glad," p. 149 in *Poems of Inspiration and Courage* by Grace Noll Crowell, copyright 1938 by Harper & Row, Publishers, Inc.; renewed 1966 by Grace Noll Crowell; for material by Margaret Applegarth from her book *Heirlooms*; for specified excerpt p. 81 from *Our Town* by Thornton Wilder, copyright © 1938, 1957 by Thornton Wilder. All selections reprinted by permission of Harper & Row, Publishers, Inc.

HOLT, RINEHART AND WINSTON, PUBLISHERS, for material from *The Raft* by Robert Trumbull. Copyright 1942, © 1970 by Robert Trumbull. Reprinted by permission of Holt, Rinehart and Winston, Publishers.

HOUGHTON MIFFLIN COMPANY for material from the works of John Burroughs, reprinted by permission of the publisher, Houghton Mifflin Company.

I DARE YOU COMMITTEE and DONALD DANFORTH, for material by William H. Danforth.

BRYSON R. KALT, for material related by his mother, Mrs. Bryson Kalt.

ART LINKLETTER, for his secret of happiness.

LITTLE, BROWN AND COMPANY, for material from *Good-bye, Mr. Chips* by James Hilton. Copyright 1934 by James Hilton. Copyright © 1962 by Alice Hilton. Used by permission of Little, Brown and Company in association with the Atlantic Monthly Press.

MRS. VINCENT LOMBARDI, for quotation by Vincent Lombardi.

MRS. KATHLEEN MARKHAM, for the poem "Outwitted" by Edwin Markham.

MCGRAW-HILL RYERSON LTD. for material from *The Collected Poems of Robert Service*. Reprinted by permission of McGraw-Hill Ryerson Limited.

ROD MCKUEN, for material from *An Outstretched Hand*, © 1980 by Rod McKuen and Montcalm Productions, published by Harper & Row, Inc.

MOREHOUSE-BARLOW COMPANY, INC., for material from *God Wants You to Be Well* by Laurence H. Blackburn, copyright © 1970. Used by permission of Morehouse-Barlow Co., Inc.

JOHN MURRAY PUBLISHERS, LTD., for excerpts from *The Spirit of St. Louis* by Charles Lindbergh. Reprinted by permission of the publisher.

GERALD L. NEES for special material.

THOMAS NELSON, INC., for material from *Today Makes a Difference* by Margueritte Harmon Bro, published by Thomas Nelson publishers.

W. W. NORTON & COMPANY, INC., for material from *Anatomy of an Illness as Perceived by the Patient* by Norman Cousins, published by W. W. Norton & Company, Inc.

MISS THEO OXENHAM, for poems "God's Sunshine" and "Are You Lonely, O My Brother?" by John Oxenham. Used by permission of T. Oxenham.

PENGUIN BOOKS LTD. for excerpts from *Our Town* by Thornton Wilder, from Thornton Wilder: Our Town & Other Plays (Penguin Plays, 1962), Copyright © Thornton Wilder, 1938, 1957. Reprinted by permission of Penguin Books Ltd.

PRENTICE-HALL, INC., for material from *How to Turn Failure Into Success* by Harold Sherman, copyright © 1958 by Prentice-Hall, Inc.; from *Let Go and Let God* by Albert E. Cliffe, copyright © renewed 1979 by Albert E. Cliffe; from *How I Raised Myself From Failure to Success in Selling* by Frank Bettger, copyright © 1977 renewed by Frank Bettger;

from *Benjamin Franklin's Secret of Success and What It Did for Me* by Frank Bettger, copyright © 1960 by Prentice-Hall, Inc.; from *Pathways to Personal Contentment* by Frank Kostyu, copyright © 1960 by Prentice-Hall, Inc. All selections published by Prentice-Hall, Inc., Englewood Cliffs, N.J.

THE PUTNAM PUBLISHING GROUP, for material from *Alone* by Richard E. Byrd. Reprinted by permission of G. P. Putnam's Sons. Copyright 1938; renewed 1966 by Richard E. Byrd.

READER'S DIGEST, for excerpts from "Wise Animals I Have Known" by Alan Devoe, *Reader's Digest*, July 1954.

PAUL W. REUTER for poem "Then Laugh" by Bertha Adams Backus and anonymous poem beginning "Give me the gift of laughter."

FLEMING H. REVELL COMPANY for material from *I Am—I Can* by Daniel Steere, copyright © 1973 by Fleming H. Revell Company; from *Finding the Way* by Dale Evans Rogers, copyright © 1969, 1973 by Fleming H. Revell Company; from *Where He Leads* by Dale Evans Rogers, copyright © 1974 by Fleming H. Revell Company; from *The Charles L. Allen Treasury* edited by Charles L. Wallis, copyright © 1970 by Fleming H. Revell Company; from *The Sermon on the Mount* by Charles L. Allen, copyright © 1966 by Fleming H. Revell Company. All selections used by permission.

MARIE RODELL-FRANCES COLLIN LITERARY AGENCY, for material from *Hill Country Harvest* by Hal Borland, published by J. B. Lippincott Co. in 1967. Reprinted by permission by Barbara Dodge Borland, Executor of the Estate of Hal Borland. Copyright © 1967 by Hal Borland.

CHARLES SCRIBNER'S SONS, a division of the The Scribner Book Companies, Inc., for excerpts from *The Spirit of St. Louis* by Charles Lindbergh. Copyright 1953 by Charles Scribner's Sons. Reprinted by permission of the publisher.

SIMON & SCHUSTER, for excerpt from *Your Prayers Are Always Answered* by Alexander Lake, copyright © 1956 by Alexander Lake. Reprinted by permission of Simon & Schuster, a Division of Gulf & Western Corporation.

DALE L. SINGER, for excerpts from his article quoting psychologist Thomas W. Allen on holistic medicine.

W. CLEMENT STONE, for material covering the secret of enthusiasm.

THE TOLEDO BLADE, for material from an editorial written by Grove Patterson.

DR. HAROLD BLAKE WALKER, for material from his article "Command the Morning."

EMORY WARD, for his statement on enthusiasm.

This book
is dedicated
in loving memory
TO
Anne B. Boardman

Contents

1

By Way of Introduction:
The Importance to You of Joy and Enthusiasm

WHAT DO YOU WANT beyond all else? Life, of course. And not merely existence, or the physical ability to breathe and function. All of us desire a particular quality of life, a combination of interest, zest, excitement, achievement, satisfaction and peace of mind. Indeed, we want to enjoy the world and the society of other people. Every individual desires to experience beauty and the highest emotions, and to possess the energy and vitality necessary to meet daily responsibilities with vigor to spare. Our hope is to live on a high level of physical strength, mental interest and spiritual meaning. And to enjoy life of this superior quality, we will discover that *joy* and *enthusiasm* are important factors in the total process.

The rationale for a book with the joint themes of joy and enthusiasm is that these two qualities are basic ingredients of the good life. And I am always interested in helping people find the good life.

By the good life, I mean one that is intensely interesting, even exciting. It is a life that is full of meaning and rich in satisfaction. Such a life is not free of difficulties or problems; of course not. But it does possess the power to overcome them and to attain victorious levels of experience.

The good life is based on a definitive value system in which joy and enthusiasm serve as both cause and effect. Desirable values are stimulated—in fact, to a considerable extent produced—by the practice of joy and enthusiasm. And, in turn, effective life-style principles definitely result in a joyous and enthusiastic manner of living. In this book, therefore, I shall present my personal treasury of joy and enthusiasm. These are incidents from thought, experience and literature, drawn from many sources, which have contributed to my own joy and enthusiasm. My purpose in assembling this material is that it may be of pleasure and value to you, and aid in developing and maintaining a positive attitude of happiness.

Those persons who consistently live by the joy and enthusiasm pattern of thinking seem to achieve a remarkable mastery over circumstances. Often I have been impressed by this fact in my relations with people.

Living the Joy Way

Many recollections come to me of persons who combined joy and enthusiasm into a quality of life that is both impressive and motivational. For example, there was the popular radio personality who invited me to be a guest on her show. It was an interview format, and I was told that the conversation would cover many subjects and be quite fast-paced.

I had never met the interviewer, but advance information revealed that she was brilliant, charming and noted for the unusual force of her personality. Accordingly, my mind envisioned a so-called glamour girl—young, beautiful and vivacious. At the radio studio I met a plain-looking woman of some sixty-plus years, walking with a decided limp (the result of a childhood disease, I later learned). She was not at all the type of person I had envisaged. She greeted me in an offhand manner and gave the impression of a rather ordinary individual. I soon became aware, however, of a strength of personality, a liveliness that was very impressive.

When we went on the air, the personal qualities of this middle-aged and handicapped woman became spectacularly evident. She exuded joy, excitement, life and enthusiasm. Her pithy comments were laced with insights and decorated with happiness. She had an infectious laugh and actually seemed to bubble over with joy. One had the impression she lived with joyous excitement and delighted in life itself.

Our conversation on the air was lively and our exchange was sheer pleasure. Finally this charming emcee said, "Well, all things come to an end, and our time has about run out, but haven't we had fun? You know something," she confided, "you and I have it made, for we live the joy way. We have enthusiasm, and with enthusiasm and joy together you really have life in full measure." So saying, she signed off her program. I have always gratefully remembered that dynamic lady who, because she "lived the joy way," had developed an indepth enthusiasm that never ran down. As a result, she was able to take in stride all the difficulties that came her way and carry on—not only joyfully—but victoriously as well.

Joy as a Therapy

The fact that this woman triumphed over physical disability underscores an important fact all too generally ignored—that the practice of joy and enthusiasm can contribute physically to therapeutic and healing benefits. The wisdom of the Bible, of course, long predated our modern psychosomatic medicine. The words "A merry heart doeth good like a medicine: but a broken spirit drieth the bones" (Proverbs 17:22) were written many generations ago. When a serious physical situation arises, the negativist glumly says, "You can't laugh that off." But perhaps you can indeed literally laugh it off by the scientific practice of joy and positive faith, joined with a deep desire to live and be well.

A thought-provoking substantiation of this point of view is impressively brought forward by Norman Cousins, a well-known editor, in his book *Anatomy of an Illness as Perceived by the Patient.* This author, who enjoys impeccable intellectual credentials, was stricken with a serious collagenic illness, a disease of the connective tissues. It was marked, so he reports, by difficulty in moving his limbs. Nodules appeared on his body like gravel under the skin, and his jaws were almost locked. A specialist gave him one chance in five hundred for full recovery. The disease may have been based on an allergy or on Cousins's inability to tolerate a toxic situation which he had experienced. The result was mental and physical tension and exhaustion. To get the adrenal glands restored to proper functioning seemed part of any possible cure. But how was Norman Cousins to get those adrenal glands, and the endocrine system in general, working well again so that health might be restored, despite the medical odds against it?

Healing Through Laughter

Cousins was familiar with Dr. Hans Selye's great book *The Stress of Life*, in which the famous Canadian physician showed that adrenal exhaustion could be caused by emotional tension such as frustration, suppressed rage and overstress. Dr. Selye, whose conclusions and findings have received international acclaim by medical and scientific leaders, detailed the effect of negative emotions on body chemistry. So the question arose in the sick man's mind: *If negative emotions produce negative chemical changes in the body, wouldn't positive emotions produce positive chemical changes?* He was unconsciously reaffirming the position stated twenty years earlier by Dr. John A. Schindler, author of *How to Live 365 Days a Year*, that what are called the "good" and "bad" emotions have corresponding effects upon physical manifestations.

Then Cousins was led to ask, "Is it possible that love, hope, faith, laughter, confidence and the will to live have therapeutic value?" Some writers had been saying for a long time that these positive factors do have such value, but they had been looked upon askance and labeled by intellectuals as superficial. But now, even though this distinguished writer knew that the turning on of positive thoughts is no simple matter, he produced a convincing corroboration of the power of the positive emotions to affect physical states. His analysis set in motion a dramatic renewal of his health and well-being.

Mr. Cousins worked out a program of laughter stimulation by watching humorous movies and reading joke books. He "made the joyous discovery that ten minutes of genuine belly laughter had an anesthetic effect and would give me at least two hours of pain-free sleep." As further proof of the healing power of self-induced joy, the patient and his physician took repeated sedimentation readings which registered scientifically that the laughter-joy procedure produced five-point drops in the sedimentation rate, and the decrease not only held but was cumulative. "I was greatly elated," concludes Mr. Cousins, "by the discovery that there is a physiological basis for the ancient theory that laughter is good medicine." And, as previously pointed out, that "ancient theory" was first referred to in the Bible: "A merry heart doeth good like a medicine: but a broken spirit drieth the bones."

Norman Cousins's experience underscores the teaching that I have been advocating for nearly half a century: that the religion of the Bible is basically scientific. It enunciates principles of mind and action which constitute formulas that will inevitably work under appropriate conditions. Indeed, Christianity may in an important sense be regarded as an exact science, for its teachings, when practiced, produce definitive results. If, for example, you hate, you will produce hate. The application of love produces love. Negative thinking brings about negative results, while positive thinking results in positive outcomes.

The human being is a mental and spiritual entity operating in a physical body. Thomas A. Edison once remarked that the basic use of the body is as a mechanism to house the brain, through which its functioning may be accomplished. It is in the brain that we consider, analyze, decide, remember, dream, aspire, believe and achieve. This being true, the rational conclusion is that the body is under the control of thinking, emotion and faith, and that this marvelous and complex physical instrument with its many involved and interlocking parts may be vitally affected by positive thinking, positive belief, positive joy and enthusiasm.

Power of Positive Thinking in Healing

United Press International released an article by Dale Singer in which he quoted psychologist Thomas W. Allen, who believes "the power of positive thinking is stronger in fighting disease than all of the technology of modern medicine." Professor Allen, of the faculty of Washington University in Saint Louis, says Singer, "preaches holistic medicine—the treatment of a patient as a whole person rather than treatment of specific symptoms of a disease." "Our thoughts reverberate in our bodies," declares psychologist Allen, who has pioneered in the use of imagery to change the way the body acts. The views of Dr. Allen and others have been supported by experiments. Cancer patients taught to use imagery techniques lived longer and better lives than their doctors had thought possible. A key point in the use of imagery to fight cancer is recognizing that cancer cells are not overpowering invaders but can be conquered. Patients who use imagery picture their immune system as victoriously aggressive and the cancer cells as relatively weak and confused. That is why radiology works; the body is bombarded and the cancer cells are overwhelmed.

Personally, I do not in any sense minimize the science of medical practice, for I believe that the doctor is a servant of God in healing. As a famous physician once said: "We treat the patient; God heals him." But I also believe it is a fact that the application of joyful, enthusiastic and positive thoughts, long and deeply held, can "bombard the body," breaking down systemic disease and helping to free the system to enjoy vitality and health.

To Feel Better, Practice Joy

The therapeutic effect of Christianity is indicated in the words of Jesus, "These things have I spoken unto you, that my joy might remain in you, and that your joy might be full" (John 15:11). Again, the Bible says, "Rejoice in the Lord alway: and again I say, Rejoice" (Philippians 4:4).

Why does the Bible teach these things? Because it is known that the best way to clear the cobwebs from the mind, to gain relief from pain, to get the blood circulating and the heart acting properly, and to keep blood pressure normal is to get joy pulsing throughout the body.

Dr. John A. Schindler said that thousands are suffering from a malady which he calls the "CDTs": cares, difficulties and troubles. Another name for it is psychosomatic illness—the effect on the body of mental states. He writes that many people are sick or below par because of an impenetrable blanket of gloom resting on their minds. When they are lifted mentally for only a few minutes daily into an area of pure joy, they can become well. No doubt that is why Jesus tells us that a way to be healthy is to cultivate joy.

"Little Bill" Miller, who coached the Cincinnati Reds, the Chicago Cubs and other teams, taught that being happy resulted in enhanced rhythm, which of course is important in athletic performance.

Teaching a tense and uptight man to play golf, the coach suggested, "Walk around the tee and sing a song." The man did so and he became relaxed and rhythmic in movement. Then he stepped up to the ball, still singing, and hit a beautiful drive.

Perhaps we do not fully realize what our religion can do for us. If you are gloomy and depressed, consciously seek God's joy. This will send a new sense of well-being coursing through your body.

Joy, flowing through the channels of consciousness, seems to affect the blood that flows to the arteries and veins. Indeed, it appears that joy effectively contributes to improved circulation. The birds are the most joyous of creatures, and they have a blood circulation that completes its circuit every two minutes. Joy steps up the chemical activity of the human body and helps pale red cells become deep red again. It is a preventive against anemia. It is amazing how many cases of illness are corrected, if not healed, by the simple application of joy. Anemia tends to be present where there is a shortage of happiness; high blood pressure is likely to appear where there is an overabundance of that which reduces happiness—monotony, anger, worry.

The more we deliberately let God shoulder the heavy responsibilities of life, the more we take life calmly and with patience, the more we can check or relieve ailments. Man, it is said, is as old as his arteries. A contributing cause of arteriosclerosis is the thinking of old defeat or frustration thoughts. A preventive, and often a help in a cure, is the inflow of new thoughts, especially light-bringing thoughts of peace, happiness and enthusiasm. Long-held hate thoughts, fear thoughts, unhappiness thoughts and other negative thoughts tend to take the spring out of life. To be healthy, it is advantageous to be religious, if the religion is love- and happiness-oriented.

Jesus said we could have joy like His own, and fullness of joy at that (John 15:11). That may be one reason why there is a significant upsurge of spiritual faith and practice today; why people are reading religious literature as never before; why increasing numbers of churches are thronged with enthusiastic people. There is, for a fact, health, vitality, new life and radiant happiness in the practice of inner joy.

And How Does One Practice Inner Joy?

It is important, first, to deal with old habit patterns. If you are a habitual negative thinker, to feel better you will need to learn to practice inner joy and thereby develop more positive attitudes. We have physical setting-up exercises; we also need spiritual setting-up exercises.

When you arise in the morning, look at yourself in the mirror; look at your face. Then for two minutes deliberately pass happy thoughts through your mind. We exercise our bodies, toning them up. Similarly, it is important to exercise the mind, just as muscles are exercised. It is in the mind that the issues of life are decided, so it must be alive and vital.

Another suggestion is to sing at least two songs every day. It has been felt by many that the best songs are religious ones, for they are positive in spirit. Learn a few hymns and sing them. As you do so, throw back your shoulders and sing with gusto. It will do you good, not only spiritually, but mentally and physically as well.

Every morning while taking your shower or bath, sing. As you wash yourself on the outside with soap and water, "wash" yourself on the inside with a spiritual song. It will stimulate cleanness and zest of mind and so contribute to your health and happiness.

To Have Enthusiasm, Practice It

Enthusiasm is one of life's greatest qualities, but it must be *practiced* to become a dominant factor in one's life.

What is the outstanding characteristic of a small child? It is enthusiasm! He thinks the world is terrific; he loves it; everything fascinates him. Thomas Huxley said that the secret of genius is to carry the spirit of the child into old age, which, of course, means never to lose your enthusiasm. But too few persons retain this excitement, and a reason is that they let enthusiasm be drained off. If you are not getting as much from life as you want, examine the state of your enthusiasm.

My mother was one of the most enthusiastic persons I ever knew. She got an enormous thrill out of the most ordinary events. She had the ability to see romance and even glory in everything. She traveled the world over and was always bursting with enthusiasm. I recall one foggy night when we were crossing from New Jersey to New York City on a ferryboat. To me, there was nothing particularly beautiful about fog seen from a ferryboat, but my mother exclaimed, "Isn't this thrilling?"

"What is thrilling?" I asked.

"Why," she replied, "the fog, the lights, the ferryboat we just passed! Look at the mysterious way its lights fade into the mist."

Just then came the sound of a foghorn, deep-throated in the heavy, padded whiteness of the mist. My mother's face was that of an excited child. I myself had felt nothing about this ride, except that I was in a hurry to get across the river.

Mother stood at the rail that night and eyed me appraisingly. She said gently, "I have been giving you advice all your life, Norman. Some of it you have taken; some you haven't. But here is a suggestion I want you to take. Realize that the world is athrill with beauty and excitement. Keep yourself sensitized to it. Love the world, its beauty and its people." I do believe that anyone trying consistently to follow that simple advice will be blessed with abundant enthusiasm and have a life full of joy. I know, for I took her advice, to my great good fortune.

"Miss Nobody"

It works for others also. For example, one night I met "Miss Nobody." After I spoke in a West Coast city, a young woman gave me a limp handshake and said in a small, timid voice, "I thought I'd like to shake hands with you, but I really shouldn't be bothering you. There are so many important people here and I'm just a nobody."

"Please remain for a few moments," I replied. "I'd like to talk with you." Later I said, "Now, Miss Nobody, let's have a little talk."

"What did you call me?" she asked in surprise.

"I called you by the only name you gave. You told me you were a Nobody. Have you another name?"

"Of course," she said. "You see, I have quite an inferiority complex. I came to hear you hoping you might say something that would help me."

"Well," I answered, "I'm saying it to you now: You are a child of

God." And I advised her to draw herself up tall each day and say aloud, "I am a child of God." I outlined some techniques for practicing enthusiasm and self-confidence.

Recently when I spoke in the same area, an attractive young woman approached me. "Do you remember me?" she asked. "I'm the former Miss Nobody." Her enthusiastic manner and the light in her eyes showed a dramatic change.

This incident underscores an important fact. You can change! Anybody can change! And even from a dull Nobody to an enthusiastic Somebody—through the practice of joy and enthusiasm.

Try the "As If" Principle

You can deliberately make yourself enthusiastic. To change yourself into whatever type of person you wish to be, first decide specifically what particular characteristic you desire to possess and then hold that image of yourself firmly in your consciousness. Then proceed to develop it by acting *as if* you actually possessed the desired characteristic, and repeatedly affirm that you are in the process of self-creating the qualities you wish to develop. In this way you are making effective use of the "As If" principle.

Often called the father of American psychology, William James (who taught this principle) said, "If you want a quality, act as if you already had it."

Shakespeare tells us in Act III of *Hamlet,* "Assume a virtue, if you have it not."

Frank Bettger, a highly successful insurance man, made effective use of this principle, as you will see in chapter 5.

Tell Yourself Good News

In developing enthusiasm, you can condition the day in the first five minutes after you awaken. Henry Thoreau, the great American writer, used to lie abed in the morning, telling himself all the good news he could think of. Then he arose to meet the day in a world filled with good things, good people, good opportunities. The practice of spiritual motivation at the start of each day will infuse you, as it did him, with new zest.

The late William H. Danforth, a prominent business leader, said: "Every morning pull yourself up to your full height and stand tall. Then think tall—think big, elevated thoughts. Then go out and act tall. Do that and joy will flow to you."

Go on spreading enthusiasm all day, and at night you will have a deposit of joy full to overflowing.

Read your Bible, for it is full of enthusiasm generators. What greater motivators, for example, are there than: ". . . all things are possible to him that believeth" (Mark 9:23), and ". . . whatsoever ye shall ask in prayer, believing, ye shall receive" (Matthew 21:22)? Saturate your mind with great passages from the Bible.

Then pray to God for guidance and get going!

(For forty life-changing Bible passages, write to the Foundation for Christian Living, Pawling, New York 12564 and ask for a free copy of my booklet *Thought Conditioners*.)

Love Life and People to Be Enthusiastic

One magic formula for successful and enthusiastic living is stated in six powerful words: *Find a need and fill it*. Every enterprise that has achieved success has been predicated on that formula.

Find people's needs; fill them. Love people. Love the sky, the hills and valleys. Love beauty, love God. The person who loves inevitably becomes enthusiastic. If you are not enthusiastic, deliberately begin today to cultivate the love of living.

Consider Fred, for example, who runs a little eating place in a big city. I went there for a late evening snack.

Resting big hands on the counter, he asked, "Okay, brother, what'll you have?"

"Are you Fred?" I asked in return.

"Yep."

"They tell me you have good hamburgers here."

"Brother, you never ate such hamburgers."

"Okay, let me have one, please."

At the counter sat an old man who looked extremely miserable. He was hunched over; his hands shook. After Fred had put my hamburger in front of me, he placed his hand in a friendly way on that of this old fellow. "That's all right, Bill," he said, "everything is all right. I'm going to fix you a bowl of that nice hot soup that you like." Bill nodded gratefully.

Another old man shuffled up to pay his check. Fred said, "Mr. Brown, watch the cars out there on the avenue. They come pretty fast at night." And he added, "Have a look at the moonlight on the river. It's mighty pretty tonight."

When I paid my check, I couldn't help remarking, "I like the way you spoke to those old men. You made them feel that life is good."

"Why not?" he asked. "Life *is* good. Me, I get a kick out of living. They're pretty sad old guys, and our place is sort of like home to them. Anyway, I kind of like 'em."

Believe in yourself and in your life. Practice the principles of enthusiasm. *Find needs and fill them* Believe that your job and, indeed, your whole life performance can be improved. Believe that you can be better than you think you are. And remember—if you think you can, you can! Bring new and bona fide enthusiasm to your life-style, for enthusiasm always makes a difference—a big difference—in your life.

The Power of Affirmation in Enthusiasm

An important technique in changing your outlook is that of affirmation. In fact, you can make almost anything of yourself by affirmation. Suppose, for example, you are full of fear. Affirm, "I'm not afraid. 'With God all things are possible' " (Matthew 19:26). The immediate effect may seem unnoticeable, but by such affirming you will have taken the first step toward courage. And if you affirm it persistently enough, your conscious mind will accept the affirmation.

If you have been apathetic and to overcome this you start affirming enthusiasm, presently it will begin to show in your new vitality. This requires self-disciplinary determination; it requires perseverance. But you can achieve a new and positive attitude. *To become* enthusiastic, *act* enthusiastic.

A help in this process of change is to develop the habit of expressing only hopeful, enthusiastic ideas. Deliberately look at the best side of things and it will become natural to expect the good, the positive. You will automatically find within yourself the enthusiasm you desire. Express enthusiasm freely and upon all occasions, and your life will strongly tend to become joyful and enthusiastic.

Walter Chrysler once said, "If I am trying to decide between two men of fairly equal ability and one man definitely has enthusiasm, I know he will go further, for enthusiasm has self-releasing power and carries all before it."

Certainly! And a person who has enthusiasm always wants to learn, so he gives the job complete interest and attention. The enthusiastic individual constantly releases maximum potential because of the outgoingness that accompanies enthusiasm.

This type of person develops spiritual and mental resources equal to his problems. This does not mean that the enthusiast will not have hard moments. He or she will even fail at times. But even so, that person will learn from failure ("failing forward," as "Boss" Charles Kettering once said) and will use failure creatively in the direction of eventual success.

Doubtless you have heard the familiar expression "If life hands you a lemon, make lemonade of it." This is another way of saying "Turn the crisis to advantage; fail forward." Enthusiasm helps you to avoid allowing problems to become overwhelming.

H. W. Arnold tells us: "The worst bankrupt is the person who has lost enthusiasm. Let one lose everything but enthusiasm and that person will again come through to success." To keep your mind and spirit full of enthusiasm, keep your intake of thought energy greater than the outgo. If you are tense and uptight, the constant tension depletes your energy and with it your enthusiasm. Therefore, utilize the spiritual and practical technique of "letting go and letting God." Ask for wisdom and guidance, and then give to your job your very best. And ". . . having done all . . . stand" (Ephesians 6:13). Leave the outcome to the Lord, trusting in His providence. In doing this calmly and confidently, you will find renewal, new energy, new enthusiasm.

Enthusiasm Changes Job Situations

Enthusiasm makes all the difference in work performance. Expose your daily occupation to apathy and your job will become difficult and tiresome. No job will go well for the person who considers it just another dull chore.

Perhaps you may say, "But my job *is* dull and there is just no future in it." But might it be that you have a dull attitude toward it? Try enthusiasm and watch it change. And see how you change with it. Enthusiasm changes a job because it changes the jobholder. When you apply enthusiasm to the job, that job comes alive with exciting new possibilities. So if you wish for a new job, try instead to apply enthusiasm to your present one and perhaps it will make that job new.

For example, ask yourself what someone else might see and do in your present job. Imagine what action he would take if suddenly he took over your job. How do you think he would react toward it? What fresh and innovative changes would he make to put new life and achievement into what you consider a dull job? Then *you* apply those ideas.

An employer told me he was going to fire an employee "out of the business." I asked, "Why not fire that person *into* the business?" He did, and the employee presently became very important to the organization. This individual was fired but not out. Enthusiasm fired him to new participation. A new personality bloomed in this worker: successful, happy, creative. Try enthusiasm on *your* job. The result can be amazing.

Enthusiasm Works Miracles in Problems

Enthusiasm is no simple or easy concept. It is a strong, rugged mental attitude that is hard to come by, difficult to maintain—but powerful.

The word *enthusiasm*, from the Greek *entheos*, means "God in you," or "full of God." So when we say that enthusiasm contains the power to work miracles in solving problems, we are actually saying that God Himself in you supplies the wisdom, courage and faith necessary to deal successfully with all difficulties. We need only to discover how to apply efficiency and right thinking enthusiastically to our problems.

Attitudes Are More Important Than Facts

Enthusiasm helps work what people describe as "miracles" in solving problems. This is because enthusiasm is an attitude of mind, and the mental attitude in a difficult situation is an important factor in its solution. Indeed, attitudes are more important than facts, for enthusiasm changes the mental outlook from fearing facts to the solid assurance that there is an answer.

These eleven words by Stanley Arnold can make an amazing difference in your thinking: *Every problem contains within itself the seeds of its own solution.*

A woman came to me at a national business convention and asked, "How may one practice what you call the magic of believing and gain the positive power of enthusiasm?"

"You might invent a method of your own for practicing that," I suggested. "You will find that it works and your enthusiasm will grow."

Here was her solution: Like many executives, she had on her desk a receptacle for incoming mail and other papers, and a second one for outgoing material. To these she innovatively added a third receptacle labeled WITH GOD ALL THINGS ARE POSSIBLE. In this she placed all papers for which she did not yet have answers. Then she added memos on problems for which no solution had been determined. To use her own phrase, she held these matters in "prayerful thinking." She said, "I surround the problems in that box with the magic of believing and the results are amazing." I was impressed by the uniqueness and workability of this ingenious method for problem solving.

Use Self-Motivators

W. Clement Stone, well-known business leader, is genuinely enthusiastic and I asked the secret of his enthusiasm.

"As you know," he answered, "the emotions are not always immediately subject to reason, but they are always immediately subject to action, mental or physical. Furthermore, repetition of the same thought or physical action develops into a habit which, repeated frequently enough, becomes an automatic reflex.

"And that's why I use self-motivators. A self-motivator is an affirmation that you deliberately use to move yourself to desirable action. You repeat a verbal self-motivator fifty times in the morning and fifty times at night for a week or ten days, to imprint the words indelibly in your memory.

"Some self-motivators are:

> For a serious personal problem: *God is always a good God!*
> For a business problem: *You have a problem . . . that's good!*
> *Within every adversity there is a seed of an equivalent or greater benefit.*
> *What the mind can conceive and believe, the mind can achieve.*
> *Find one good idea that will work and . . . work that one idea!*
> *Do it now!*
> *To be enthusiastic . . . act . . . enthusiastically!"*

The Contagion of Enthusiasm

"Enthusiasm, like measles, mumps and the common cold, is highly contagious," says the writer Emory Ward.

But, unlike measles and mumps and colds, enthusiasm is good for you. Hope you catch it—and good.

When contagious, enthusiastic faith in yourself releases you from the self-built prison of your mind, then you begin to change, and as you change, your whole life also changes. You are set free to live on a level never before experienced.

Perhaps you are being overwhelmed by problems. When they have you disorganized and confused, remember there is Someone concerned about you. The Lord will help you to turn about, rethink clearly and overcome. Your victories will fill you with enthusiasm and joy. Your problems will give way before enthusiasm and positive faith.

One night Mrs. Peale and I were invited to dinner in a very fashionable apartment on New York's Park Avenue. In fact, we were told that our host was one of the richest men in the world. I never did learn whether that was so, but the home was indeed palatial. One walked on thick carpets; the decorations were exquisite, the hangings lovely. All kinds of jade and vases and Chinese art were displayed. However, my chief interest (because finally it was getting close to nine o'clock) was the dinner. At long last, the hostess, with some embarrassment, announced to the twenty guests that the cook had become indisposed, and therefore there wasn't going to be any dinner served there. But she had made arrangements with a nearby restaurant, and we would all go there.

So we all piled into taxicabs and went. The restaurant turned out to be one of those gloomy, dark (but high-class) places where you have to grope your way to a table through flickering candlelight. I had never been in this place before; in fact I had never heard of it. As we were being seated I asked my wife, "What is this joint?" In a whisper she said, "Don't show your ignorance. This is a night club."

Well, my acquaintance with night clubs is very limited, but the dinner must have been satisfactory. I couldn't see what I was eating but suffered no ill effects. After dinner it was announced that a floor show was coming on. I said to my wife, "Let's get out of here."

She replied, "You can't; it wouldn't look right."

"But," I persisted, "they wouldn't even see us if we left."

"Well," she said, "you've got to stay and say good-bye to your hostess in a proper way."

I suggested, "I'll leave her a note."

But my wife was firm. "No. Stay here with me."

And I am certainly glad that I did remain, because a woman came on to sing. I became deeply impressed by this woman. She wore a long, black dress that had no shape to it; she had no jewelry or any other kind of adornment. And she wasn't very beautiful (at least she wasn't so beautiful you would write home about her). She was a very plain person and I figured her age at about fifty to fifty-five. I said to my wife, "I thought they had only young-appearing glamour girls in these places."

She replied, "This woman is supposed to be one of the greatest."

"Well," I remarked, "she has to prove it to me."

Then she started to sing. She was French, and she sang some of her songs in French and others in English, the latter with a delightful French accent. She captivated everyone. She seemed to sort of reach out and hug all those people to herself with love. She threw herself, body, mind and soul, into her singing. She sang as if it were the last time on earth she would ever sing. She sang as though that was the greatest thing in the world, and she lifted me right out of my seat. Here was a woman who loved what she was doing; who didn't particularly care how she looked. Now, maybe that's good or maybe it's bad, but it doesn't make all that much difference. She rose above appearance; she was a believer in life. She loved life, and she made everybody else love it. She was filled with enthusiasm and a joy that is unforgettable to me now, years later, as I write about it.

Zest for Life

It is important to live with zest even in the midst of life's troubles.

In the office of a large business organization, the head of the firm radiated exuberance and confidence. When I arrived, he was in conference with his chief assistant. As they discussed a problem, I could do no other than listen to their conversation. The talk was positive and enthusiastic. It was a refreshing, stimulating and upbeat treatment of a problem.

I asked, "How do you explain your zest and positive thinking? You two are alive, really alive, and you have confidence that you can handle a tough problem."

One of them leaned across the table and said, "Remember those words, 'I can do all things through Christ who strengthens me'? [Philippians 4:13 NKJB]. Well, we believe that. We don't talk about it, but that is the source from which we derive faith in ourselves and our ability to handle our problems."

"And so you are joyful and enthusiastic. Is that it?" I asked.

"That's it," said both of them. They had zest and enthusiasm and so they attracted zest and enthusiasm. Life does give back in kind.

"Let Enthusiasm Take Hold!"

I knew the late Vince Lombardi, the famous football coach. When he went to Green Bay, he faced a defeated, dispirited team. He stood before the men, looked them over silently for a long time, and then in a quiet but intense way said, "Gentlemen, we are going to have a great football team. We are going to win games. Get that. You are going to learn to block. You are going to learn to run. You are going to learn to tackle. You are going to outplay the teams that come against you. Get that.

"And how is this to be done?" he continued. "You are to have confidence in me and enthusiasm for my system. The secret of the whole matter will be what goes on up here." And he tapped his temple. "Hereafter, I want you to think of only three things: your home, your religion, and the Green Bay Packers, in that order! Let enthusiasm take hold of you—beginning now!"

The players sat up straight in their chairs. "I walked out of that meeting," said the quarterback, "feeling ten feet tall!" That year the team won seven games—with virtually the same players who had lost ten games the year before. The next year they won a division title and the third year the world championship. Why? Because, added to hard work and skill and love of the sport, enthusiasm made the difference.

What happened to the Green Bay Packers can happen to an individual. What goes on in the mind is what determines the outcome. When a person gets real enthusiasm, it can be seen in the flash of the eyes, in an alert and vibrant personality. You can observe it in the spring of the step. You see it in the verve of the whole being. Enthusiasm makes the difference in attitude toward other people, toward the job, toward the world. It makes a big difference in the joy of human existence.

Are you vibrantly alive? Do you possess contagious enthusiasm? God the Father wants to give you the Kingdom, so that you will have joy in life. Jesus said, ". . . because I live, ye shall live also" (John 14:19). And He meant life abundant and overflowing.

Joy and Enthusiasm Can Remake Your Life

The kind of living that makes life good is as exact as a science, and not something that you muddle through without rules. Life responds to certain precise methods and procedures. Your life can be either a hit or a miss, empty or full, depending on how you think and act. The enthusiast knows and draws upon valid resources. He plays it cool and straight. Such a person believes there is nothing in life so difficult that it can't be overcome; that faith can indeed move mountains. It can change people. It can change the world. It can help you survive all the great storms in your life.

However, joy and enthusiasm are qualities that must be affirmed and reaffirmed, practiced and repracticed. Donald Curtis suggests that you affirm each morning:

I move serenely forward into the adventure of life today. I am filled with inspiration and enthusiasm. I am guided and protected by the Infinite in everything I say and do. I project confidence and authority. I am sure of myself in every situation. With God's help, I am filled with the strength and energy to be what I am and to do what I have to do. . . .

Walk in Newness of Life

Activate your mind so that it becomes alive and vital. Heed the Bible, which tells us to "walk in newness of life" (Romans 6:4). That is a powerful thought. We are not to think old, dead, dull and desultory thoughts. Walk in newness of life, in a quality of life that is new every morning and fresh every evening—always exciting and joyful.

The Bible glows with excitement and enthusiasm. It is well called the Book of Life. "And be renewed," it says, "in the spirit of your mind" (Ephesians 4:23)—not merely on the surface of your mind, but in the deep spirit that activates your thoughts.

Joy and enthusiasm can remake your life! This book was assembled to help you think and live the joy way, the enthusiasm way.

Ten Steps to a Joyful and Enthusiastic Life

Since thinking has much to do with what your life becomes, you might consider the following suggestions:

FIRST   Stop depreciating yourself. There is a lot that is *right* in you. Empty your mind of failure thoughts and mistakes and start seeing yourself as a competent person.

SECOND   Eliminate self-pity thoughts. Start thinking of what you *have*, instead of dwelling on what you may have lost. List your assets of personality and talent.

THIRD   Quit thinking constantly of yourself. Think of *others*. Actually go out and look for someone who needs the kind of help you can give, and then give it freely. You will not maintain a continuing flow of abundance if your thoughts are only of yourself.

FOURTH   Remember the words of Goethe: "He who has a firm will molds the world to himself." Almighty God put a tough power into human beings called the *will*. Use it.

FIFTH   Have a *goal* and put an achievable timetable on it.

SIXTH   Stop wasting your mental energy on gripes and post-mortems, and start thinking about what to do *now*. Amazing things happen when you think constructively.

SEVENTH   Every morning and every evening articulate these words aloud: "I can do all things through Christ who strengthens me."

EIGHTH   Every day say three times: "This is the day the Lord has made. I will rejoice and be glad in it" (adapted from Psalms 118:24).

NINTH   Think and practice joy every day.

TENTH   Get enthusiasm; think enthusiasm; live enthusiastically!

2

Life Can Be a Joyous Adventure

LIFE CAN BE A JOYOUS adventure every day all the way. The word *adventure* suggests something rather big and special, but life as a joyous adventure need not be "a big deal." It can move forward daily in the simple things that comprise most of our life experience.

Henry van Dyke states the matter quite well, I think. The great writer and preacher says:

> To be glad of life, because it gives you the chance to love and to work and to play and to look up at the stars; to be satisfied with your possessions, but not contented with yourself until you have made the best of them; to despise nothing in the world except falsehood and meanness, and to fear nothing except cowardice; to be governed by your admirations rather than by your disgusts; to covet nothing that is your neighbor's except his kindness of heart and gentleness of manner; to think seldom of your enemies, often of your friends and every day of Christ; and to spend as much time as you can with body and with spirit, in God's out-of-doors— these are the little guideposts on the footpath of peace.

These "little guideposts on the footpath of peace," practiced daily, add up finally to a totality of joy and enthusiasm. Both of these desirable qualities are developed through a constant cultivation of goodness, appreciation and love. Add to this the habit of consciously living with God, and joy wells up within your heart and your mind bursts with enthusiasm. The joy of life has become yours.

Mother Teresa of Calcutta, who received the 1979 Nobel Peace

Prize for her selfless devotion to India's teeming multitudes of the poor, is considered by many a living saint. In her book *A Gift for God*, she shows how joy is simply to try to carry out God's will in the common way of daily experience:

> Joy is prayer—Joy is strength—Joy is love—Joy is a net of love by which you can catch souls. She gives most who gives with joy.
>
> The best way to show our gratitude to God and the people is to accept everything with joy. A joyful heart is the inevitable result of a heart burning with love.
>
> We all long for heaven where God is but we have it in our power to be in heaven with Him right now—to be happy with Him at this very moment. But being happy with Him now means:
> loving as He loves,
> helping as He helps,
> giving as He gives,
> serving as He serves,
> rescuing as He rescues,
> being with Him for all the twenty-four hours,
> touching Him in His distressing disguise.

When one loves and gives and helps and serves in the manner so touchingly suggested by Mother Teresa, then joy deepens and enthusiasm for God's world and its people measurably increases. And the result is that life becomes good—very good indeed. Its meaning and purposes are enhanced. One rejoices to be alive.

And God's sunshine will keep going, as John Oxenham describes it in a charming poem:

GOD'S SUNSHINE
Never once since the world began
    Has the sun ever stopped his shining.
His face very often we could not see,
And we grumbled at his inconstancy;
But the clouds were really to blame, not he,
    For, behind them, he was shining.

And so--behind life's darkest clouds
  God's love is always shining.
We veil it at times with our faithless fears,
And darken our sight with our foolish tears,
But in time the atmosphere always clears,
  For his love is always shining.

If we pass through every day with the thought of joyous adventure, if we are activated by decent motives, and at all times treat people in a kindly manner, we will feel good about ourselves and the love of life will grow. As Rod McKuen says:

I measure success by how well I sleep on a given night. If I have not had to question my motives for any particular action I might have undertaken, or knowingly caused another human being trouble or discomfort, then I am at peace with my God and myself and I fall asleep easily.

If sleep comes hard, then I know the day has been a personal failure.

I have personally put Rod's principle to the test by letting my mind run over the day as I lie down to sleep. If I can honestly feel that I have been motivated by right purposes and that my relationships with my family, friends and all others I have met have been loving and caring, then it is amazing how fast I can go off to sleep and what a good night I have. And this has much to do with starting off the next morning on another adventure of joyous living.

Of course I realize that life in its course brings us face to face with hardship, pain, illness and difficulties of one kind or another. This is the way our years on earth are made. The wise Creator, it appears, wants to make strong people of us, and no one can become strong without struggle with adversity, resistance and problems. Struggle makes us strong, and in the process of overcoming, we achieve happiness. We learn thereby how, despite everything, life can become a joyous adventure.

Let me tell you about a husky, active fifteen-year-old high school athlete in Indiana who dove into a pond and broke his neck. He was pulled from the water but has not walked since. The swimming accident paralyzed his arms and legs and confined him to a wheelchair, perhaps for the rest of his days.

Needless to say, life almost stopped for this hitherto vigorous and very alive boy. In a situation like that it could be easy to settle for defeat, to give up in despair. But Gerald Nees was not made of weak stuff. He was strong in mind and strong in character.

One thing he was determined to do was to graduate from high school. Needing just one credit to complete the requirement, he told his mother he planned to take an art course.

"But how will you do that?" she asked. "Your hands cannot move." Undaunted, he showed her how he could draw with a pencil between his teeth. Being a strong mother of a strong son, she encouraged him to take the course, and a new life began for him.

Becoming seriously interested in art, Gerald was granted a partial art scholarship by the University of Minnesota. Then he received a full scholarship from the Famous Artists School in Connecticut, where he learned to work with oils. With infinite patience, he paints the things of beauty he sees around him, holding a brush in his mouth. Many of his paintings depict the farmland scenes of his home. Living with his mother on a fifty-acre farm worked by his brother-in-law, he helps to support the family through his paintings.

Gerald has exhibited in a number of one-man art shows. His first one was sponsored by W. Clement Stone, who purchased fourteen paintings himself. We had some of Gerald's paintings on display at the Foundation for Christian Living in Pawling, New York, and as I looked at them I myself was inspired by this remarkable man.

It is amazing how a person, no matter how handicapped, can create and release dynamic forces that turn back defeat. Gerald Nees's rebound capacity, his faith in God, his comeback power, his ability to stand up to his adversity, brought him through the crisis. Loving life, he refused to take defeat, and he is putting a lot into life every day.

"I guess I'm kind of ornery," says Gerald. "I don't like pity and I don't give it. I like living and I want to live as long as I can, because I don't want to miss anything. I feel good—I feel happy."

There are two possible attitudes to take when things go hard. One is to let it throw you, to become discouraged, even hopeless, to give up and to let go the feeling that you can do something about it. That attitude is, of course, disastrous. For if you admit—even to yourself—that you do not have what it takes to cope with adversity, your personal resources will not come into action. And those personal resources are amazing in their potential.

Almighty God put into each one of us that power called *spiritual resource*, and, if we keep it alive, cultivate it, activate it, step it up, when the crisis comes, we may draw upon it. Therefore, in addition to never giving up, the secret is to draw hard and deep on your inherent spiritual resources.

The person who possesses a strong faith in God is the most fortunate of all people, for that individual has resources to depend on.

> The Lord is good, a strong hold in the day of trouble; and
> he knoweth them that trust in him.
>
> Nahum 1:7

Actually, though stormy weather may be less than pleasant, storms are not all that bad if we know how to meet them—and even turn them to our advantage. And of course the best and simplest method is just to stand up to them with courage and dogged persistence added to the faith that you are never alone. Or as Rod McKuen says:

> Never fear being alone, because you never are.

I like the story and the philosophy of storms expressed by a rugged old-time cowboy who said he had learned life's most important lesson from Hereford cows. All his life he had worked cattle ranches where winter storms took a heavy toll among the herds. Freezing rains whipped across the prairies. Howling, bitter winds piled snow into enormous drifts. Temperatures might drop quickly to below-zero degrees. Flying ice cut into the flesh. In this maelstrom of nature's violence, most cattle would turn their backs to the icy blasts and slowly drift downwind, mile upon mile. Finally, intercepted by a boundary fence, they would pile up against the barrier and die by the scores.

But the Herefords acted differently. Cattle of this breed would instinctively head into the windward end of the range. There they would stand shoulder to shoulder facing the storm's blast, heads down against its onslaughts. "You most always found the Herefords alive and well," said the cowboy. "I guess that is the greatest lesson I ever learned on the prairies—just face life's storms."

The lesson is a valid one. Do not attempt to evade things you are afraid of, or difficulties; don't go drifting with the wind, trying to keep away from them. Every human being has to decide again and again, and still again, whether to meet fearsome difficulties head-on or to try running away.

Actually, you can never outrun fear; nor can you outrun adversity. Try that unequal race and you will run yourself down, a pathetic victim of the inevitable. Try a better way. Stand up to your troubles and stormy times, remembering always that they are removable.

In this day when walking, jogging, running and bicycle riding are popular with a nation of health-conscious citizens, the philosophy of a bicycle rider says something about how to think when the going gets hard and thereby to keep the joyous adventure spirit in one's mind:

> Those who ride bicycles say that it is easier to ride up a hill at night than it is during daylight. Hills that are practically impossible of ascent may be negotiated at night. At night the cyclist can see but a few feet in front of him, and the faint light of his lantern gives him the illusion that the hill is either level or not steep. He feels that he can go the few feet more than his light shows, and in this manner keeps on and on, while in the daytime he sees the whole hill, the whole problem, and it seems so steep to climb that his courage fails him.
>
> AUTHOR UNKNOWN

It is a fact that joy comes out of difficulty, perhaps even more certainly than out of fortuitous circumstances. As I think of the truly joyful people I have known, almost without exception the happiest are those who found their joy either in spiritual experience, or in difficulty, or in both.

Harold Blake Walker tells it truly:

Trouble is no disaster when we know we can manage it. Indeed, the joy of Jesus came not from the absence of difficulty, but from a conviction of power to triumph. What a day it is for a boy learning to swim when he comes up from a ducking with a sputtering shout: "Look, Dad, I'm swimming!" It isn't the absence of problems that brings joy to a man struggling to build a little business on Main Street; it is the grateful assurance of capacity for victory affirmed in the gleeful word to his wife: "Honey, we're solvent."

What brings joy to the morning isn't the thought that today will be free from problems, or difficulties or troubles, but rather the knowledge that "I can do all things in him who strengthens me." A man I know in the hospital understands that. He is a tonic when I see him, snared as he is with arthritis and a bad heart. He greets me with a grin that stretches from ear to ear and even when he feels the worst he has some cheerful word. He knows from long years of comradeship with God that he is spiritually adequate for anything that may come.

The well-known writer Margueritte Harmon Bro gives us some good, ancient Japanese wisdom:

One of the most famous of the sixteenth-century shogun rulers of Japan, Tadaoki Hosakaw, was asked one day by his senior statesman, "What sort of man do you call an able man?"

"An able man is like an oyster in the Bay of Akashi."

"You are right," the senior statesman said, pleased at his master's wisdom.

The men around them looked blank. One of them said, "We really cannot comprehend the oyster which seemed so to satisfy your highness."

The statesman explained: "The Bay of Akashi is one of the most stormy of all bays, so that fierce waves toss and toughen the oyster shells until it is known that the best shells come from that bay of violence. So, in the world of men, the best men have been tried in continual storms of adversity."

One of the great sources of joy in the adventure of life is the wonderful feeling that we have what it takes to overcome—our fears, our problems, our adversities, even pain and death.

Life is out there, shouting at you what it is going to do to you. Face it, love it, live it! Just remember who you are—you are a child of the eternal God; you are a disciple of Jesus Christ. And stand up to death, knowing that nothing can ever destroy you, for you have life that is forever new. So go forward with confidence.

We cultivate joy in the experience of trouble. We also may cultivate it by practicing it, by learning to laugh and be glad. We finally become what we think and what we do. Therefore, if we want to live a joyous life, we will do well to act joyfully. And one way to do so is just to laugh.

Bertha Adams Backus gives some good advice about laughter as a way to joy:

THEN LAUGH

Build for yourself a strong box,
    Fashion each part with care;
When it's strong as your hand can make it,
    Put all your troubles there;
Hide there all thought of your failures,
    And each bitter cup that you quaff;
Lock all your heartaches within it,
    Then sit on the lid and laugh.

Tell no one else its contents,
    Never its secrets share;
When you've dropped in your care and worry
    Keep them forever there;
Hide them from sight so completely
    That the world will never dream half;
Fasten the strong box securely—
    Then sit on the lid and laugh.

A poet whose name I do not know prayed for the gift of laughter in the midst of trouble. And to have the ability to live joyously is to

make life an exciting adventure regardless of how many dark valleys
we must traverse.

> Give me the gift of laughter, oh, I pray,
> Though tears should hover near;
> Give me the gift of laughter for each day—
> Laughter to cast out fear.
>
> With hope to greet the coming of each dawn,
> And faith that never dies;
> Give me the gift of laughter, oh, I pray—
> Laughter instead of sighs.

But I would like to reiterate that the ability just to hang in there, to
stick with it through storm and hard going, is to come out with joy. I
have the pleasure of knowing the famous writer A. J. Cronin, and I
admire him greatly as an author who has entertained and inspired
millions. But he got his training the hard way. The joyous adventure
of life for him came down some rough roads. If life goes hard for
you, read the following. I have read this story for my soul's good half
a hundred times or more:

THE TURNING POINT OF MY LIFE

I was 33 at the time, a doctor in the West End of London. I
had been lucky in advancing through several arduous Welsh
mining assistantships to my own practice—acquired on the
installment plan from a dear old family physician who, at our
first interview, gazed at my cracked boots and frayed cuffs,
and trusted me.

I think I wasn't a bad doctor. My patients seemed to like
me—not only the nice old ladies with nothing wrong with
them, who lived near the Park and paid handsomely for my
cheerful bedside manner, but the cabbies, porters and dead-
beats in the mews and back streets of Bayswater, who paid
nothing and often had a great deal wrong with them.

Yet there was something ... though I treated everything

that came my way, read all the medical journals, attended scientific meetings, and even found time to take complex postgraduate diplomas ... I wasn't quite sure of myself. I didn't stick at anything for long. I had successive ideas of specializing in dermatology, in aural surgery, in pediatrics, but discarded them all. While I worked all day and half of most nights, I really lacked perseverance, stability.

One day I developed indigestion. After resisting my wife's entreaties for several weeks, I went casually to consult a friendly colleague. I expected a bottle of bismuth and an invitation to bridge. I received instead the shock of my life: a sentence to six months' complete rest in the country on a milk diet. I had a gastric ulcer.

The place of exile, chosen after excruciating contention, was a small farmhouse near the village of Tarbert in the Scottish Highlands. Imagine a lonely whitewashed steading set on a rain-drenched loch amid ferocious mountains rising into gray mist, with long-horned cattle, like elders of the kirk, sternly munching thistles in the foreground. That was Fyne Farm. Conceive of a harassed stranger in city clothes arriving with a pain in his middle and a box of peptonizing powders in his suitcase. That was I.

Nothing is more agonizing to the active man than enforced idleness. A week of Fyne Farm drove me crazy. Debarred from all physical pursuits, I was reduced to feeding the chickens and learning to greet the disapproving cattle by their Christian names. Casting around desperately for something to do, I had a sudden idea. For years, at the back of my mind, I had nursed the vague illusion that I might write. Often, indeed, in unguarded moments, I had remarked to my wife, "You know, I believe I could write a novel if I had time," at which she would smile kindly across her knitting, murmur, "Do you, dear?" and tactfully lead me back to talk of Johnnie Smith's whooping cough.

Now, as I stood on the shore of that desolate Highland loch I raised my voice in a surge of self-justification: "By Heavens! This is my opportunity. Gastric ulcer or no gastric ulcer, I will write a novel." Before I could change my mind I walked straight to the village and bought myself two dozen penny exercise books.

Upstairs in my cold, clean bedroom was a scrubbed deal table and a very hard chair. Next morning I found myself in this chair, facing a new exercise book open upon the table, slowly becoming aware that, short of dog-Latin prescriptions, I had never composed a significant phrase in all my life. It was a discouraging thought as I picked up my pen and gazed out the window. Never mind, I would begin. Three hours later Mrs. Angus, the farmer's wife, called me to dinner. The page was still blank.

As I went down to my milk and junket—they call this "curds" in Tarbert—I felt a dreadful fool. I recollected, rather grimly, the sharp advice with which my old schoolmaster had goaded me to action. "Get it down!" he had said. "If it stops in your head it will always be nothing. Get it down." And so, after lunch, I went upstairs and began to get it down.

Perhaps the tribulations of the next three months are best omitted. I had in my head clear enough the theme I wished to treat—the tragic record of a man's egoism and bitter pride. I even had the title of the book. But beyond these naive fundamentals I was lamentably unprepared. I had no pretensions to technique, no knowledge of style or form. I had never seen a thesaurus. The difficulty of simple statement staggered me. I spent hours looking for an adjective. I corrected and recorrected until the page looked like a spider's web, then I tore it up and started all over again.

Yet once I had begun, the thing haunted me. My characters took shape, spoke to me, laughed, wept, excited me. When an idea struck me in the middle of the night I would get up, light a candle, and sprawl on the floor until I had translated it to paper. At first my rate of progress was some 800 labored words a day. By the end of the second month it was a ready 2000.

Suddenly, when I was halfway through, the inevitable happened. Desolation struck me like an avalanche. I asked myself: "Why am I wearing myself out with this toil for which I am so preposterously ill-equipped?" I threw down my pen. Feverishly, I read over the first chapters which had just arrived in typescript from my secretary in London. I was appalled. Never, never had I seen such nonsense in all my life. No one would read it. I saw, finally, that I was a presumptuous lunatic, that all I had written, all that I could ever write was wasted effort, sheer futility. Abruptly, furiously, I bundled up the manuscript, went out and threw it in the ash can.

Drawing a sullen satisfaction from my surrender or, as I preferred to phrase it, my return to sanity, I went for a walk in the drizzling rain. Halfway down the loch shore I came upon old Angus, the farmer, patiently and laboriously ditching a patch of the bogged and peaty heath which made up the bulk of his hard-won little croft. As I drew near, he gazed up at me in some surprise: he knew of my intention and, with that inborn Scottish reverence for "letters," had tacitly approved it. When I told him what I had just done, and why, his weathered face slowly changed, his keen blue eyes scanned me with disappointment and a queer contempt. He was a silent man and it was long before he spoke. Even then his words were cryptic.

"No doubt you're the one that's right, doctor, and I'm the one that's wrong. . . ." He seemed to look right to the bottom of me. "My father ditched this bog all his days and never made a pasture. I've dug it all *my* days and I've never made a pasture. But pasture or no pasture," he placed his foot dourly on the spade, "I canna help but dig. For my father knew and I know that if you only dig enough a pasture can be made here."

I understood. I watched his dogged working figure with rising anger and resentment. I was resentful because he had what I had not: a terrible stubbornness to see the job through at all costs, an unquenchable flame of resolution brought to the simplest, the most arid duties of life. And suddenly my trivial dilemma became magnified, transmuted, until it stood as the timeless problem of all mortality—the comfortable retreat, or the arduous advance without prospect of reward.

I tramped back to the farm, drenched, shamed, furious, and picked the soggy bundle from the ash can. I dried it in the kitchen oven. Then I flung it on the table and set to work again with a kind of frantic desperation. I lost myself in the ferociousness of my purpose. I would not be beaten, I would not give in. I wrote harder than ever. At last, toward the end of the third month, I wrote *finis*. The relief, the sense of emancipation, was unbelievable. I had kept my word. I had created a book. Whether it was good, bad or indifferent I did not care.

I chose a publisher by the simple expedient of closing my eyes and pricking a catalogue with a pin. I dispatched the completed manuscript and promptly forgot about it.

In the days which followed I gradually regained my health, and I began to chafe at idleness. I wanted to be back in harness.

At last the date of my deliverance drew near. I went around the village saying good-by to the simple folk who had become my friends. As I entered the post office, the postmaster presented me with a telegram—an urgent invitation to meet the publisher. I took it straight away and showed it, without a word, to John Angus.

The novel I had thrown away was chosen by the Book Society, dramatized and serialized, translated into 19 languages, bought by Hollywood. It has sold millions of copies. It altered my life radically, beyond my wildest dreams . . . and all because of a timely lesson in the grace of perseverance.

But that lesson goes deeper still. Today, when the air resounds with shrill defeatist cries, when half our stricken world is wailing in discouragement: "What is the use . . . to work . . . to save . . . to go on living . . . with Armageddon round the corner?" I am glad to recollect it. The door is wide open to darkness and despair. The way to close that door is to go on doing whatever job we are doing, and to finish it.

The virtue of all achievement, as known to my old Scots

farmer, is victory over oneself. Those who know this victory can never know defeat.

A. J. CRONIN

And, I might add, they also know the joyous adventure of life.

Knowing Dr. Cronin's strong Christian faith, I am sure he was buttressed in his struggles by great words like those found in Deuteronomy 31:6, words that will see you through most difficulties:

> Be strong and of a good courage, fear not, nor be afraid of them: for the Lord thy God, he it is that doth go with thee; he will not fail thee, nor forsake thee.

One thing that must be overcome if your life is to be a joyous adventure is fear and its components of worry and anxiety. A medical doctor asked me recently how often, during a year of sermons and speeches, I gave a talk against fear. He added that if he were a speaker or writer he would be out there fighting fear most of the time. "If we could cut down the incidence of fear, worry and anxiety, I could get in a lot more games of golf, for fear is basically what keeps my office filled up with patients," he said with a smile.

The late Dr. Smiley Blanton, famous psychiatrist, said: "Anxiety is the great modern plague." But he added that anxiety can be eliminated by the practice of healthy thinking and by developing a strong faith. Indeed, Dr. Blanton and I together once wrote a book entitled *Faith Is the Answer*. So never minimize fear, worry or anxiety. The English word *worry* is derived from an old Anglo-Saxon word which meant to strangle or to choke. Long-held worry, on the basis of this definition, results in a strangulation of life. And therefore life can hardly be a joyous adventure if it is based on a mental attitude of fear.

Here is what some thinkers have to say about fear:

> There is perhaps nothing so bad and so dangerous in life as fear.

JAWAHARLAL NEHRU

Fear is the most devastating of all human emotions. Man has no trouble like the paralyzing effects of fear.

PAUL PARKER

The only thing we have to fear is fear itself.

FRANKLIN D. ROOSEVELT

Fear is the sand in the machinery of life.

E. STANLEY JONES

They can conquer who believe they can. He has not learned the first lesson of life who does not every day surmount a fear.

RALPH WALDO EMERSON

Fear makes the wolf bigger than he is.

GERMAN ADAGE

Faith in yourself and faith in God are the key to mastery of fear.

HAROLD SHERMAN

And to all of these wise statements about fear as a chief enemy of joyous adventure, let me add an even greater one:

For God hath not given us the spirit of fear; but of power, and of love, and of a sound mind.

2 Timothy 1:7

What a combination: power—love—a sound mind. With a life so constituted, you can walk under the sun and the stars unafraid. And have the time of your life all your life.

I rather like the "sound mind" attitude expressed by Frank Bettger, one of America's greatest salesmen:

I wrote an article on "When You Are Scared, Admit It!" in 1944 for *Your Life* magazine. Shortly after it was published I was thrilled to receive the following letter:

Somewhere in the Pacific
September 11, 1944

Dear Frank Bettger:

I have just finished reading and thinking over an article by you in the September issue of Your Life *magazine. You entitled your article "When You Are Scared, Admit It!" and I have been thinking over just how good that advice is—especially out here as a soldier in a combat area.*

I have naturally had experiences similar to those you relate. Public speeches in high school and in college; conferences with employers before and after obtaining a job; the first serious talk with that certain young woman—all these have caused me to be scared, and greatly so.

Well perhaps you wonder why I write to you from out here to second your statements because certainly I'm not giving public speeches or asking for a job. No, I'm not subjected to ordeals from that direction, but believe me I do know what fear is and how it affects a person. And also, we have found that your advice, "Admit it!" is absolutely just as appropriate and right when you are facing a Jap demon assault.

It has been proven time and time again out here that the men who fail to admit their fear are the ones who crack in battle. But if you admit you are scared, damned scared, and don't try to fight it down, then you are on the right road to overcoming your fear in most cases.

And now, thank you for writing that article, and I sincerely hope that those lucky students and workers who have the opportunity to make use of your advice will certainly do so.

Sincerely,
CHARLES THOMPSON

This letter from out there in the firing line was certainly written under the most dire circumstances, yet, there are probably people right now, reading this chapter, who have walked up and down time and time again in front of a man's office door, trying to get up enough courage to go in. Are you one of them? Big men—their wives don't tremble in their presence! You pay a big compliment to a man when you tell him you are scared in his presence.

There is no disgrace in admitting you are scared, but there is disgrace in failing to *try*. So whether you're talking to one person, or a thousand, if that strange demon fear, public enemy number one, suddenly steals up on you, and you find yourself too scared for words, remember this simple rule:

When You're Scared, Admit It.

I once gave a sermon in a church in London and told the congregation how in-depth faith can cast out fear. The late British industrialist Arthur Rank was present and afterward asked me if I knew of his "Wednesday Worry Club." I replied that I had heard of it but would he tell me more about this ingenious device.

Lord Rank pointed out that Christianity is a commonsense teaching, one that works when worked. Therefore we can outwit fear by innovative procedures. For example, he told me that there were thirteen steps from the ground level to his office. Every morning he would "say a little prayer" on each of those steps as he mounted them.

Daily some worry or anxiety would arise. Instead of permitting the worry to disturb him then, he wrote it on a slip of paper and deposited it in a box to be worried about on Wednesday at 4:00 P.M. When that time came, the "Wednesday Worry Club" would meet and he would open the box, only to find that practically all of the worries collected there had been handled or were no longer important. "In fact," he declared, "I would find that about ninety-two percent of my worries had failed to materialize."

"But what did you do about the eight percent?" I asked.

"Oh," he laughed, "I just put them back in the box to be worried about next Wednesday afternoon."

Ralph Waldo Emerson had the same sensible understanding:

> Some of your hurts you have cured,
> And the sharpest you still have survived,
> But what torments of grief you endured
> From evils that never arrived!

Laurence H. Blackburn, my longtime friend, for whom life was always a joyous adventure, gives some good advice about handling fear effectively:

Everyone is afraid of something, either admitted or unconfessed. Some fears have been brought out into the open and recognized for their universality, as well as the damage they do. There is the fear of any unsettling situation that may make us less sure of ourselves; a rut is so comfortable, after all! And what if we should be exposed for the person we really are? Then there might come disregard or humiliation or ridicule. Some find it unbearable to contemplate any change within or without. The fear of failure makes us inadequate to meet the tests of life; the fear of poverty keeps us poor; the fear of people fends off those who would be our friends; the fear of dying fills every living hour with the haunt of death. Add to these scores of others, like the fear of old age, the fear of the dark—as well as your own pet fears.

What shall we do about our fears?

Instead of denying them, or hiding them, or running away from them, why not face our fears to see what they really are?

Direct action is recommended as a most effective remedy, too. If you handle your fears one by one with decisiveness and courage, you will find that they will shrivel into less significance. You will be the master over them. You will be free. How wise were Emerson's words: "He has not learned the lesson of life who does not every day surmount a fear."

The cure for fear is Faith.

Make use of great affirmations. Put them on your desk, your mirror, or over the kitchen sink. Keep them in your mind. Repeat them at every odd moment during the day. Say them over and over before you go to sleep. You know many to use, but here are some suggested affirmations. Make your own list and use them daily as adversaries of fear:

The Lord is my shepherd (Psalms 23:1).

When I am afraid, I put my trust in thee (Psalms 56:3 RSV).

I sought the Lord, and he answered me, and delivered me from all my fears (Psalms 34:4 RSV).

The world will make you suffer. But be brave! I have defeated the world! (John 16:33 TEV).

By practice you can develop your faith into assurance. Put your fears into God's hands—and leave them there! His care of us in our yesterdays gives us faith that He will take care of us today.

Dr. W. R. Maltby describes the disciples of Jesus Christ, who, knowing the score about life's tough realities, were also victoriously joyous:

> In the Sermon on the Mount, Jesus promised his disciples three things—that they would be entirely fearless, that they would be absurdly happy, and that they would get into trouble. They did get into trouble and found, to their surprise, that they were not afraid. They were absurdly happy, for they laughed over their own troubles and only cried over other people's.

Let us sum up this matter of fear and worry by the two following quotations from the wisest of all books, the Bible:

> Do not worry about tomorrow; it will have enough worries of its own. There is no need to add to the troubles each day brings.
>
> Matthew 6:34 TEV

> For I the Lord thy God will hold thy right hand, saying unto thee, Fear not; I will help thee.
>
> Isaiah 41:13

With those ideas as guiding lights, any one of us can go far toward making life a joyous adventure.

Perhaps this down-to-earth poem says it all:

WORRY
Ain't no need to worry
    about the things to come
Forget about your problems
    and face them one by one.

Ain't no need to worry
    about what might have been
Just trust the Heavenly Father
    and let that be the end.
Ain't no need to worry
    about things unknown to you
Have faith in God and rest assured
    that He will see you through.

EARLINE ROSS COLE

3
The Gift of Life

I HAVE OFTEN WONDERED why certain writers, speakers and leaders are remembered forever. For their ability, leadership qualities and achievements, of course, but one important reason is their boundless enthusiasm and the joy they took in life and in the world.

Moby Dick, for example, is an unforgettable story, and its author, Herman Melville, whose life span was from 1819 to 1891, is an unforgettable character. His imagination seemed to tingle with life and with the charm and fascination of the world. Here is an example of his extraordinary ability to express his enthusiasm:

> Standing at the masthead of my ship during a sunrise that crimsoned sky and sea, I once saw a large herd of whales in the east, all heading towards the sun, and for a moment vibrating in concert with peaked flukes.
>
> As it seemed to me at the time, such a grand embodiment of adoration of the gods was never beheld, even in Persia, the home of the fire worshippers.
>
> As Ptolemy Philopator testified of the African elephant, I then testified of the whale, pronouncing him the most devout of all beings. For according to King John, the military elephants of antiquity often hailed the morning with their trunks uplifted in the profoundest silence.

Sensitivity to life in all its varied and incredible forms is to be expected, especially when amazement and wonderment are awakened. But sensitivity to the marvelous privilege of responding to life's simple things is perhaps a more profound indicator of joy and enthusiasm.

One March morning I went to breakfast in a motel in a midwestern city. The coffee shop was crowded and I stood in the doorway surveying the room for a vacant table. Then I noticed a table for two by a window where a stranger was seated. He waved to me to come over and invited me to sit with him.

He was a very pleasant person and had a remarkably cheerful attitude for a dark, dreary, windy, rainy March morning. In fact, he was quite enthusiastic. A gust of wind drove a hail of raindrops against the window and the rain ran down in fast-moving rivulets on the windowpane. "I get a great kick out of March," he observed, "with its wild winds. They seem to sigh around the house whispering mysteriously. And just look at those big raindrops hanging like jewels on the bare branches of that bush out there."

Then he noticed the steam rising from the coffee. "Don't you like to see steam coming up from food on a table?" he asked. "It's like home, somehow. Anyway, it's great to be alive, and what a day we're going to have."

"My friend," I said, "you are full up with poetry, romance, aliveness and enthusiasm, and that is what I like to see in a person. But how did you get this way?"

He told me he was in a serious automobile accident and hung for some weeks between life and death. Once, from seemingly afar off, he heard an attendant in the hospital say of him, "I don't think this one will make it." Then, what seemed long ages later, a kindly man in a white coat looked down at him and said quietly, "You are going to live; you are going to get well and be okay."

"You cannot possibly imagine the delicious sense of life that surged in me at those words," said my table companion. "Like a condemned prisoner, I had a reprieve; the sentence of death was lifted. And ever since I've had a sharp and distinct awareness of the wonder and glory of the simple things—like wind, and rain, and steam, and sunlight."

I sat entranced by this wonderful man who thrilled me with a new joy and enthusiasm for that great gift—the gift of life—and for the beautiful world with its dear old, simple, everyday blessings.

Thomas Curtis Clark writes of them with sensitivity:

GOD GIVE ME JOY

God give me joy in the common things:
In the dawn that lures, the eve that sings.

In the new grass sparkling after rain,
In the late wind's wild and weird refrain;

In the springtime's spacious field of gold,
In the precious light by winter doled.

God give me joy in the love of friends,
In their dear home talk as summer ends;

In the songs of children, unrestrained;
In the sober wisdom age has gained.

God give me joy in the tasks that press,
In the memories that burn and bless;

In the thought that life has love to spend,
In the faith that God's at journey's end.

God give me hope for each day that springs,
God give me joy in the common things!

And David Grayson (pen name for Ray Stannard Baker) gets the
common glory even more down to earth:

Blessed is the man who can enjoy the small things, the
common beauties, the little day-by-day events; sunshine on
the fields, birds on the bough, breakfast, dinner, supper, the
daily paper on the porch, a friend passing by. So many people
who go afield for enjoyment leave it behind them at home.

Great Possessions

Of course we would expect wise Ralph Waldo Emerson to have
something good to say on this subject, and he does. The following
quotation is given to every person who appears on "The Alan

McGirvan Radio Show" in Brisbane, Australia. Alan gave one each
to my wife and me when we were guests on his sprightly program
recently:

> To laugh often and much;
>   to win the respect of
> intelligent people and the
>   affection of children;
> to earn the appreciation of honest
>   critics and endure the betrayal of
>   false friends;
>   to appreciate beauty;
>
> to find the best in others; to leave
>   the world a bit better, whether by
> a healthy child, a garden patch or
>   a redeemed social condition;
>
>   to know even one life
>   has breathed easier because
>   you lived.

> This is to have succeeded.

Life, even with all its woes, frustrations and difficulties, is still a
wonderful experience.

Part of the problem concerning our attitude toward life is, perhaps, that we tend to shut our eyes to its qualities of beauty and excitement. Our senses may be dulled to the excitement all about us
every day, wherever we may be. Simply to be able to hear and see
the glory in the everyday is one of the most unused yet important of
all skills.

Lorado Taft says it pointedly:

> We are living in a world of beauty, but few of us open our
> eyes to see it!
>
> What a different place this world would be if our senses
> were trained to see and to hear!
>
> We are the heirs of wonderful treasures from the past:
> treasures of literature and of the arts. They are ours for the

asking—all our own to have and to enjoy, if only we desire them enough.

I often think of Saint Francis of Assisi when reflecting on insensitivity to the beauty and wonderment in common things. This saint in his youth was the rather roistering son of a nobleman. But later he had a profound spiritual awakening and as a result became one of the most lovable characters of history.

I seem to recall a story about him that says a lot about the type of person he was. One day, so the story goes, he said to a monk, "Let us go to the village square and preach." But instead of talking, he patted a dog in the town, helped a poor woman across a street, stopped to comment on the beauty of a weed. He spoke most kindly to all the people they passed in their walk around the square and then the two headed for home. "But, master," said the monk, "we came to preach."

"We have done so, my son," said the saint. "We just went about loving people, and dogs, and life. That was of itself a sermon."

In fact, it is said of Francis that, so happy was he, he was known to "preach" to the cattle and the birds, telling them how wonderful life is and how much God loved them as well as all of us. This sheer delight in the wonder of life is reflected in the following prayer in which he hails the sun as his brother and the moon as his sister:

O Most High, Almighty, Good Lord God, to Thee belong praise, glory, honor and all blessing.

Praised be my Lord God, with all His creatures, and especially our brother the Sun, who brings us the day and who brings us the light: fair is he, and he shines with a very great splendour.

O Lord, he signifies us to Thee!

Praised be my Lord for our sister the Moon, and for the Stars, the which He has set clear and lovely in the heaven.

Praised be my Lord for our brother the Wind, and for air and clouds, calms and all weather, by which Thou upholdest life and all creatures.

Praised be my Lord for our sister Water, who is very serviceable to us, and humble and precious and clean.

Praised be my Lord for our brother Fire, through whom

Thou givest us light in the darkness; and he is bright and pleasant and very mighty and strong.

Praised be my Lord for our mother the Earth, the which doth sustain us and keep us, and bringeth forth divers fruits and flowers of many colors, and grass.

Praised be my Lord for all those who pardon one another for love's sake, and who endure weakness and tribulation: blessed are they who peacefully shall endure, for Thou, O Most High, will give them a crown.

Praised be my Lord for our sister, the Death of the Body, from which no man escapeth. Woe to him who dieth in mortal sin. Blessed are those who die in Thy most holy will, for the second death shall have no power to do them harm.

Praise ye and bless the Lord, and give thanks to Him and serve Him with great humility.

This wonder of life, which we sense in the simple things all about us, is further demonstrated in another marvelous thing that we often take for granted as ordinary. The human body, which we use every minute in life, is likewise one of the world's wonders, as is pointed out by Margaret Applegarth:

Here you sit, held together by a fabulous interweaving of flexible muscles and tendons and cartilages, all comfortably tucked inside an enormous envelope called skin, which in turn is made up of literally billions of cells, each busy every blessed second wearing out, eliminating, and then building up.

Yet you take your incredible body for granted, unless something goes wrong.

Even the Psalmist centuries ago noticed. "I am fearfully and wonderfully made."

Part of the wonder is that you have so little fear. Rarely do you remind your pulse: "For heaven's sake, beat!" Or your heart: "Did you pump? Did you count it? How often per minute? Five quarts a moment, I hope. Seventy-five an hour, remember!" Or to each little drop of blood: "Are you taking your exciting excursion trip through 169 miles of my canal-

ways and blood vessels in three minutes?" Or to your eyelids:
"Did you blink? And are my tear ducts sluicing off the dust
from my eye-balls regularly?"

Best of all, how blest you should feel that instead of making
you embarrassingly tall to contain the thirty-five to forty feet
of tubes inside your intestinal and kidney tracts, your Creator
cleverly looped them into a neat little twenty cubic inches.

It might be well, therefore, to say to your brain, "Ponder!"
For your body is a temple made for worship and thanksgiving, and you have much for which to be profoundly grateful
every moment of every day that you dare live so carefree of
all these details.

So even those things, and even people who annoy and situations
that frustrate and irritate, may be put in proper perspective as we
contemplate the beauty and wonder of life and the world and God.
The following anonymous verse says it quite well, I think:

> God—there are things in my life I don't like,
>   Folks I can't bear;
> But there are more things I would hate to change,
>   Friends I can't spare.
> So when you hear me complaining aloud,
>   Just turn away;
> Deep inside my ungracious heart, I am
>   Grateful each day. *Amen.*

As we hope to grow in wisdom while walking along the pathway
of life, we may acquire the basic philosophy and faith expressed by
Margaret E. Sangster:

> To bluest skies that arch the way
> I lift my thankful eyes to-day.
> The sunlight pours a golden tide
> O'er airy forest, green and wide;
> Pure odors drift the morning through,
> And God has led me hitherto.

> What bliss to take His guiding hand
> To trust, if not to understand;
> To rest through change and toil and tears
> On Him whose grand eternal years
> In ever living youth are new
> And cry, "He leads me hitherto."

That philosophy and faith may stand us in good stead in times of crisis. And crisis may come when least expected, which makes the development of faith all the more important:

HE'S WITH ME

Storm clouds and strong gusts of wind had come up suddenly over Columbus, Ohio. The Alpine Elementary School radio blared tornado warnings. It was too dangerous to send the children home. Instead, they were taken to the basement, where the children huddled together in fear.

We teachers were worried too. To help ease tension, the principal suggested a sing-along. But the voices were weak and unenthusiastic. Child after child began to cry—we could not calm them.

Then a teacher, whose faith seemed equal to any emergency, whispered to the child closest to her, "Aren't you forgetting something, Kathie? There is a power greater than the storm that will protect us. Just say to yourself, 'God is with me now.' Then pass the words on to the child next to you."

As the verse was whispered from child to child, a sense of peace settled over the group. I could hear the wind outside still blowing with the same ferocity of the moment before, but it didn't seem to matter now. Inside, fear subsided and tears faded away.

When the all-clear signal came over the radio sometime later, students and staff returned to their classrooms without their usual jostling and talking.

Through the years I have remembered those calming words. In times of stress and trouble, I have again been able to find release from fear or tension by repeating, "He's with me now."

PHYLLIS I. MARTIN

Nature, its varied aspects and moves, its grandeur and pastoral serenity, has an enormous influence on life as an experience of peace, inspiration and wonder. Some of our encounters with nature are memorable and, indeed, unforgettable. For example, I remember a time years ago in the China Sea. The ocean was smooth, even limpid, and the ship glided almost silently save for the far-off rumble of the engines and a wash at the stern. A mist lay over the vast deep and the silvery moon rays filtered through what seemed a gossamer curtain. Life may be said to be a collection of such jewel-like memories fastened on the string of the years.

Another memory is of dusk at an observation point on the rim of the Grand Canyon, when the slanting, sinking sun quickly changed the reds and golds of the peaks and minarets of the canyon into purple shadows and night fell across the desert. Meanwhile, in a chance encounter there, the greatest authority on the Grand Canyon, John C. Merriam, discussed the antiquity and still-continuing evolution of the vast abyss.

Still another memory that will linger across the years is a leisurely ramble I took through the noble aisles and arches of Sherbrooke Forest in Victoria, Australia. Dwarfed by the aged and enormous eucalyptus trees that soared perhaps two hundred feet, we wandered in a silence almost primeval. And yet it was not absolute silence, for presently the ear became tuned to the immense activity of the forest as it went about its designed functioning. But the long shafts of sunlight, occasional clouds floating high above, the smell of the good earth, the buzz of insects, the profound serenity, left a healing memory of the wonder of the world.

When I think of these things my mind goes to Robert Service, the poet of the Alaska ice peaks, of the Yukon's turbulent blue waters, of the great silences of the lofty mountains. Here are lines from his compelling poem, "The Spell of the Yukon":

> I've stood in some mighty-mouthed hollow
> That's plumb-full of hush to the brim;

I've watched the big, husky sun wallow
　　In crimson and gold, and grow dim,
Till the moon set the pearly peaks gleaming,
　　And the stars tumbled out, neck and crop;
And I've thought that I surely was dreaming,
　　With the peace o' the word piled on top.

Everything in the great northland of the continent was dear to Robert Service. Its beauty charmed and thrilled him; its rugged power inspired him. Its effect was almost beyond words, but still his glorious speech caught and held this wonder of life:

The summer—no sweeter was ever;
　　The sunshiny woods all athrill;
The grayling aleap in the river,
　　The bighorn asleep on the hill.
The strong life that never knows harness;
　　The wilds where the caribou call;
The freshness, the freedom, the farness—
　　O God! how I'm stuck on it all.

All my life long I have read and quoted Robert Service. In a bookshop in New York on February 20, 1925, I bought a little book by William L. Stidger called *Giant Hours With Poet Preachers*, and in that volume I first met Service. I've traveled to Alaska and to the Yukon and on starlit nights have read again his inspired words from the poem "The Three Voices":

For the stars throng out in their glory,
　　And they sing of the God in man;
They sing of the mighty Master,
　　Of the loom his fingers span,
Where a star or a soul is a part of the whole
　　And weft in the wondrous plan.

Here by the camp fire's flicker,
　　Deep in my blanket curled,
I long for the peace of the pine gloom,

> Where the scroll of the Lord is unfurled,
>   And the wind and the wave are silent,
>   And the world is singing to world.

And Service also is a devotee of the simple, strong, beautiful things that mark the glory of the world, the wonder of life. For he writes in praise of them: "The simple things, the true things, the silent men who do things. . . ." He was a gold seeker, as many were in those far-back, heroic days of America's youth. But he found a fairer gold even than shining metal. He found gold tinged with glory:

> There's gold, and it's haunting and haunting;
>   It's luring me on as of old;
> Yet it isn't the gold that I'm wanting
>   So much as just finding the gold.
> It's the great, big, broad land 'way up yonder,
>   It's the forests where silence has lease;
> It's the beauty that thrills me with wonder,
>   It's the stillness that fills me with peace.
>   *The Spell of the Yukon*

Despite all the pain, difficulty and tragedy of human existence, life—just plain life itself—remains a wonderful thing. So much so that with the Psalmist we may say:

> O praise the Lord, all ye nations: praise him, all ye people.
> For his merciful kindness is great toward us: and the truth of
> the Lord endureth for ever. Praise ye the Lord.
>   Psalms 117

And to make it truly great, I have long advocated my own practice of quoting every morning aloud these dynamic, life-stimulating words:

> This is the day which the Lord hath made; we[I] will rejoice
> and be glad in it.
>   Psalms 118:24

None of the things we have said must be taken to indicate that life, wonderful as it is, will be altogether sweetness and light. There are in its structure not a few disappointments, troubles and sorrows. But the person who believes in life in its totality and in its various aspects will be one who shares the faith expressed by Ella Wheeler Wilcox:

FAITH

I will not doubt, though all my ships at sea
    Come drifting home with broken masts and sails;
    I shall believe the Hand which never fails,
From seeming evil worketh good to me;
      And, though I weep because those sails are battered,
      Still will I cry, while my best hopes lie shattered,
        "I trust in Thee."

I will not doubt, though all my prayers return
    Unanswered from the still, white realm above;
    I shall believe it is an all-wise Love
Which has refused those things for which I yearn;
      And though, at times, I cannot keep from grieving,
      Yet the pure ardor of my fixed believing
        Undimmed shall burn.

I will not doubt, though sorrows fall like rain,
    And troubles swarm like bees about a hive;
    I shall believe the heights for which I strive,
Are only reached by anguish and by pain;
      And, though I groan and tremble with my crosses,
      I yet shall see, through my severest losses,
        The greater gain.

I will not doubt; well anchored in the faith,
    Like some stanch ship, my soul braves every gale,
    So strong its courage that it will not fail
To breast the mighty, unknown sea of death.
      Oh, may I cry when body parts with spirit,
      "I do not doubt," so listening worlds may hear it
        With my last breath.

Life can indeed be wonderful and replete with joy and enthusiasm when you have a positive and reasonable attitude toward yourself and your job. A bit of solid philosophy by an old-time big league baseball player has long struck my fancy. It is by Bobby Doerr, one-time Boston Red Sox star and also a member of nine All-Star teams and a participant in the World Series:

> It seems to me that what any man's beliefs are depends upon how he spends his life. I've spent a good part of mine as a professional baseball player and the game that I play for a living is naturally a very important thing to me. I've learned a lot of things on the baseball diamond about living—things that have made me happier and, I hope, a better person. I've found that when I make a good play and take my pitcher off the hook, it's just natural for me to feel better than if I made a flashy play that doesn't do anything except make me look good for the grandstands. It works the same way off the ball field, too. Doing a good turn for a neighbor, a friend, or even a stranger gives me much more satisfaction than doing something that helps only myself. It's as if all people were my teammates in this world and things that make me closer to them are good, and things that make me draw away from them are bad.
>
> Another belief very important to me is that I am only as good as my actual performance proves that I am. If I cannot deliver, then my name and reputation don't mean a thing. I thought of this when in the spring of 1951 I told my team that I would not play in 1952. I reached this decision because I realized that I wouldn't be able to give my best performance to the people who would pay my salary by coming through the turnstiles. I don't see how anyone can feel right about success or fame that is unearned. For me, most of the satisfaction in any praise I receive comes from the feeling that it is the reward for a real effort I have made.
>
> Many ball players talk a lot about luck and figure that it is responsible for their successes and failures, on and off the field. Some of them even carry around a rabbit's foot and other good-luck charms or they have little rituals that they go

through to make sure of things going the way they want them to. I've never been able to go along with people who believe that way. I've got a feeling that there's something much deeper and more important behind the things that happen to me and whether they turn out good or bad. It seems to me that many of the things which some people credit to luck are the results of divine assistance. I can't imagine an all-wise, all-powerful God that *isn't* interested in the things I do in my life. Believing this makes me always want to act in such a way as to deserve the things that the Lord will do for me.

Maybe that's the most important thing of all. Doing good in order to deserve good. A lot of wonderful things have happened to me in my lifetime. I've had a long, rewarding career in organized baseball. The fans have been swell to me and I've always liked my teammates. But what really matters is that I've got just about the best folks that anyone could ask for. Doing what I can to make things more pleasant for my father and mother and for my wife and our son has been one of the things I have enjoyed most because it seems to be a way for me to pay back something of what I owe them for all the encouragement and pleasure they've given me.

I guess the best way to sum it all up is that I'm happy to be around and I'd like to be able to make other people glad of it, too.

To enjoy the wonder of living and to experience true pleasure, we must never give up, never falter, but always keep on keeping on. Many years ago Frank L. Stanton wrote a poem called "Keep a-Goin'" and to do that is to keep joy and enthusiasm alive:

> If you strike a thorn or rose,
>   Keep a-goin'!
> If it hails or if it snows,
>   Keep a-goin'!
> 'Taint no use to sit an' whine
> When the fish ain't on your line;
> Bait your hook an' keep a-tryin'—
>   Keep a-goin'!

When the weather kills your crop,
   Keep a-goin'!
Though 'tis work to reach the top,
   Keep a-goin'!
S'pose you're out o' ev'ry dime,
Gittin' broke ain't any crime;
Tell the world you're feelin' *prime*—
   Keep a-goin'!

When it looks like all is up,
   Keep a-goin'!
Drain the sweetness from the cup,
   Keep a-goin'!
See the wild birds on the wing,
Hear the bells that sweetly ring,
When you feel like singin', sing—
   Keep a-goin'!

The amazing power inherent in human beings to keep going despite disaster is poignantly illustrated in the life experience of Elena Zelayeta. I was a guest for dinner in her home in San Francisco and it was a delightful evening. The dinner itself would have made the evening memorable, but the sparkling personality of our hostess was the truly memorable experience.

There were many courses, each one a masterpiece, in this typical Mexican dinner. As each course came on, its history and how it was made was explained to us, for Elena is an expert in Mexican cooking. She had cooked this dinner herself—and she is totally blind.

This amazing woman once ran a beautiful and very successful restaurant in San Francisco. As she was sitting alone at home one day the telephone rang. She groped her way to it to hear a voice saying: "Your husband has been in an accident. I must tell you that he is dead."

Blind—and now suddenly her husband had been taken. Struggling in her darkness, she reached for the help of Almighty God. She told me that one day in that darkness she felt as though a great hand took hold of her own and lifted her up. She began to live a wonderful life. She traveled the West Coast speaking to audiences, demonstrating her cooking on the stage, cooking with the senses of taste and smell and touch. "After all," she says, "that is what cooking is about. You don't need to see."

That night I asked her, "What is your secret?"

Her answer was priceless: "Always act as if the impossible were possible."

Years ago I found a little book entitled *I Dare You* by William Danforth. It seems that when Danforth was a young boy he was in delicate health and it was supposed he would not live long, that he wouldn't be able to keep going. The story of how he developed positive faith and lived to a great age has long impressed me.

One day at school a teacher who frequently gave the boys some strong talk on health singled out young Danforth and said to him, "I dare you to become the healthiest boy in this class." Now practically every boy in the class was a real husky compared with Will. But the teacher said to him: "I dare you to chase those chills and fevers out of your system. I dare you to fill your body with fresh air, pure water, wholesome food and daily exercise until your cheeks are rosy, your chest full and your limbs sturdy. I dare you to become the healthiest boy in this class."

Will Danforth took the dare—and he developed a splendid, robust physique. Seventy years after that time, in the lobby of the Jefferson Hotel in Saint Louis, where I had a little visit with him, I asked, "Mr. Danforth, just what did you do to get strong?" And so enthusiastic was he that despite his age he proceeded to show me all his exercises right there in the lobby of the hotel and insisted that I follow the exercises myself!

We soon had an audience of about twenty-five people around us. He said to them, "Everyone can be strong." And they believed it. And I believe it. He told me that he had outlived every member of his class. Dare to be strong! And determine to keep going!

Mr. Danforth tells about a salesman named Henry. This salesman came to him one morning and said, "Mr. Danforth, I've had it. I never can be a salesman. I haven't got the nerve. I haven't got the ability. You shouldn't be paying me the money I receive. I feel guilty taking it. I'm quitting right now."

Mr. Danforth looked at him and said, "I refuse to accept your resignation. I dare you, Henry, to go out right now today and do the biggest sales job that you've ever done. *I dare you.*"

He writes that he could see the light of battle suddenly blaze up in the man's eyes—the same surge of determination which he himself had felt when that teacher years before dared him to become strong and healthy. The salesman simply turned and walked out. That evening he came back and laid down on Mr. Danforth's desk a collection of orders showing that he had, in fact, made the best record of his life. And the experience changed him permanently. He surpassed his own record many times in the years that followed. Positive faith can always keep you going with joy and enthusiasm, living life at its best.

Finally, in talking about the fact that life is wonderful, I just want to say that I think people are wonderful. I once asked Art Linkletter the secret of his happiness, for he is truly a happy man. His answer was "Interest and curiosity." He said, "Will Rogers said he never met a man he didn't like. I have never met a person who didn't interest me." Thornton Wilder would agree:

> Now there are some things we all know . . . . We all know that *something* is eternal. And it ain't houses, and it ain't names, and it ain't earth, and it ain't even stars—everybody knows in their bones that *something* is eternal, and that something has to do with human beings. All the greatest people ever lived have been telling us that for five thousand years and yet you'd be surprised how people are always losing hold of it. There's something way down deep that's eternal about every human being.
>
> *Our Town*

4
More Power to You

"MORE POWER TO YOU," said a man whom I casually encountered in an airport. It was said only in passing and is a remark frequently heard. But for some reason, I continued to reflect upon it and what possible meaning it had for me. That we do need more power is obviously a fact: power to do the job, to keep going, to stand up to and rise above difficulties. Without such power, life can be pretty bleak and discouraging. But with inner power of mind and spirit it can be quite the contrary. Life will then take on victorious results and accordingly joy and enthusiasm.

I well recall one of the first times I experienced the relationship of power to joy and enthusiasm. As a very young minister in Brooklyn, New York, I was asked to give a brief invocation at a meeting scheduled to be held in Prospect Park on Memorial Day. I prepared the few sentences of a short prayer. On arrival at the speaker's stand I looked out at a crowd estimated at fifty to sixty thousand people. Examining the printed program, I was astonished and aghast to note that I was listed not for an invocation but rather for an "address." Immediately I was overcome with fear and the strong negative thought that no way could I meet this unexpected assignment. I was prepared only for a short prayer, not for an address to such a large crowd. Nervously I went to the presiding official, the late Brigadier General Theodore Roosevelt, Jr., son of President "Teddy" Roosevelt, and timidly called his attention to the error. He looked at me speculatively. "You *are* a minister, aren't you?" I nodded.

"What's the matter, son? You surely are not afraid." He pointed toward a section of the crowd reserved for the mothers of service men and women who had died. "As a representative of God I know you have something to say to those sad and grieving mothers. You can do it. More power to you."

The way in which he talked to me and his encouraging punch in the chest did something to me, and while the program was in progress, I put together a talk designed especially to comfort and strengthen those mothers. When I sat down after my speech General Roosevelt said, "What did I tell you? You rang the bell. You had the power going for you." Well, I knew full well that my ringing of the bell was pretty faint but all of a sudden I was full of happiness—and new enthusiasm for reaching and helping people welled up within me. And, needless to say, I loved General Roosevelt until the day he died on the beaches of Normandy.

Power is available to meet difficult situations. And this power is built into us by the Creator. It is there waiting to be called upon, to be summoned forth, and it can help us through many a crisis. This fact should give rise to joy and stimulate an abounding enthusiasm.

Victor Hugo gives a bit of wise advice:

> Be like the bird
> That, pausing in her flight
> Awhile on boughs too slight,
>   Feels them give way
> Beneath her and yet sings,
> Knowing that she hath wings.

One of the greatest of all spiritual principles is expressed in the phrase, "Let go and let God." He is the basic, the true Power. The principle is to do all you can about a problem in the way of thought, study, discussion and prayer. Then, as Saint Paul says, ". . . having done all . . . stand" (Ephesians 6:13). When you have done all that you possibly can, what more can be done by you? It is then that one is wise to let God take over. Trust Him to handle the situation, for He has the know-how, and since He is deeply interested in you as His child, He will produce for you a good result. And it will surely be a good result, for He Himself is good and does all things right and well.

One of the great spiritual writers of the past hundred years was a devout and gifted woman by the name of Hannah Whitall Smith, whose book *The Christian's Secret of a Happy Life* is a classic. One section of the book deals with the matter of leaving your burdens with the Lord:

I knew a Christian lady who had a very heavy temporal burden. It took away her sleep and her appetite, and there was danger of her health breaking down under it. One day, when it seemed especially heavy, she noticed lying on the table near her a little tract called "Hannah's Faith." Attracted by the title, she picked it up and began to read it, little knowing, however, that it was to create a revolution in her whole experience. The story was of a poor woman who had been carried triumphantly through a life of unusual sorrow. She was giving the history of her life to a kind visitor on one occasion, and at the close the visitor said feelingly, "Oh, Hannah, I do not see how you could bear so much sorrow!" "I did not bear it," was the quick reply; "the Lord bore it for me." "Yes," said the visitor, "that is the right way. We must take our troubles to the Lord." "Yes," replied Hannah, "but we must do more than that: we must *leave* them there. Most people," she continued, "take their burdens to Him, but they bring them away with them again, and are just as worried and unhappy as ever. But I take mine, and I leave them with Him, and come away and forget them. If the worry comes back, I take it to Him again; and I do this over and over, until at last I just forget I have any worries, and am in perfect rest."

My friend was very much struck with this plan, and resolved to try it. The circumstances of her life she could not alter, but she took them to the Lord, and handed them over into His management; and then she believed that He took it, and she left all the responsibility and the worry and anxiety with Him. As often as the anxieties returned, she took them back, and the result was that, although the circumstances remained unchanged, her soul was kept in perfect peace in the midst of them. She felt that she had found out a practical secret; and from that time she sought never to carry her own burdens, nor to manage her own affairs, but to hand them over, as fast as they arose, to the Divine Burden-bearer.

This same secret, also, which she had found to be so effectual in her outward life, proved to be still more effectual in her inward life, which was in truth evermore utterly unmanageable. She abandoned her whole self to the Lord, with all that she was and all that she had, and, believing that He took that which she had committed to Him, she ceased to fret and worry, and her life became all sunshine in the gladness of belonging to Him. It was a very simple secret she found out: only this, that it was possible to obey God's commandment contained in those words, "Be careful for nothing; but in everything by prayer and supplication, with thanksgiving, let your requests be made known unto God"; and that in obeying it, the result would inevitably be, according to the promise, that the "peace of God which passeth all understanding shall keep your hearts and minds through Christ Jesus."

And when that deep peace of God that passes understanding comes to us, then we do indeed have great joy and enthusiasm.

The effect of faith applied to the problems of life is astonishing—amazing—in its power. In a newspaper column about interesting phenomena I read of a professor who performed an amazing demonstration. His equipment consisted of a board, a large nail, a bottle and a very small fleck of carborundum. He took the bottle in his right hand—it was a big, thick, heavy bottle, one of the thickest, heaviest bottles obtainable—and he used it as a hammer. With a series of powerful strokes of the bottle he drove the nail into the board. This did not fragmentize the bottle, break it, crack it or chip it—so strong was that bottle. Then the professor took the tiny fleck of carborundum, which is one of the hardest of the solids, and dropped it into the glass bottle, which instantly shattered into many pieces. It wasn't size or amount that did it; rather, it was essence.

So it is with the problems and difficulties of this life. Suppose you bring to bear against your difficulties all the force and power that you can muster, all the struggling that you can manage, all the resisting of which you are capable, but it isn't effective. Then take a mustard-seed pinch of faith and drop it with confidence into the problem. The problem shatters, breaks apart; all the elements of the problem are revealed and you can put it together for a solution.

Faith of the in-depth variety that goes beyond mere intellectual assent produces joy and enthusiasm that no adversity or trouble can diminish. The late Governor Charles Edison of New Jersey told me of the resilient, undefeatable spirit of his father, the famous inventor Thomas A. Edison.

On the night of December 9, 1914, the great Edison industries of West Orange were virtually destroyed by fire. Thomas Edison lost 2 million dollars that night and much of his life's work went up in flames. He was insured for only $238,000, because the buildings had been made of concrete, at that time thought to be fireproof.

Thomas Edison's son was twenty-four; Thomas was sixty-seven. The young man ran about frantically, trying to find his father. Finally he came upon him, standing near the fire, his face ruddy in the glow, his white hair blown by the December winds.

"My heart ached for him," Charles Edison told me. "He was sixty-seven—no longer a young man—and everything was going up in flames. He spotted me. 'Charles,' he shouted, 'where's your mother?' 'I don't know, Dad,' I said. 'Find her,' he bade me. 'Bring her here. She will never see anything like this again as long as she lives.' "

The next morning, walking about the charred embers of all his hopes and dreams, Thomas Edison said, "There is great value in disaster. All our mistakes are burned up. Thank God we can start anew."

And three weeks after the fire, his firm delivered the first phonograph. That is the story of a man who faced the inevitable hazards of human existence with fortitude, courage, faith. He knew that sixty-seven years meant nothing, that the loss of money meant nothing, because he could always build again.

There is generally someone about who always will say, "But Thomas A. Edison was a very unusual man. He could take it that way. I couldn't."

Yes, Edison was unusual. But I have seen many people, unknown to fame and fortune, who were also unusual in the same way; people who thought right, acted right and believed right under the adversity which comes to every human being. Through faith you can be victorious over anything this world can do to you. The Bible promises that. ". . . In the world ye shall have tribulation: but be of good cheer;

I have overcome the world" (John 16:33). And you can too, if you have positive faith.

Never let anything get you down, no matter how difficult, how dark, how hard it is, how hopeless it may seem, how utterly depressed you may become. Whatever the nature of the circumstances involved, never let anything get you down. Always there is help and hope for you.

In Switzerland I was having dinner with some friends in an ancient inn called the *Chesa Veglia*, at Saint Moritz in the Upper Engadine Valley. This inn is some four hundred years old. The Swiss and Germans have a curious custom of carving interesting sentiments on the interior walls of such places. And some old chalets have inspiring legends carved or painted on the outside walls. On the dining room wall in the *Chesa Veglia* I saw this inscription written in German:

> *Wenn du denkst es geht nicht mehr,*
> *Kommt von irgendwo ein lichtlein her.*

In English this reads:

> When you think everything is hopeless,
> A little ray of light comes from somewhere.

That wise saying is about four hundred years old. When you think everything is hopeless, always remember, a little ray of light comes from somewhere.

Where is this somewhere? Inside your own mind, of course. You may feel hopeless—but Almighty God has established Himself in you, and nothing is hopeless.

A great poet wrote, "Hope springs eternal in the human breast." Whenever you feel that things are getting you down, remember, there is a little ray of hope, of light, that comes from somewhere. It comes from God, of whom it is said, "With men this is impossible; but with God all things are possible" (Matthew 19:26). And Jesus also said, "Remember, I will be with you forever" (Matthew 28:20 paraphrased). So, if darkness has settled in your mind, just open it up and let in that little ray of light that comes from somewhere.

Edison, it would seem, as he viewed that fire, was the kind of person Joseph Addison had in mind when he wrote:

> The grand essentials to happiness in this life are something to do, something to love, and something to hope for.

There is a curious thing about happiness and enthusiasm in that these qualities can exist and grow and dominate, even in the midst of trouble and difficulty. This interesting thought is expressed by William George Jordan:

> Happiness is the greatest paradox in Nature. It can grow in any soil, live under any conditions. It defies environment. It comes from within; it is the revelation of the depths of the inner life as light and heat proclaim the sun from which they radiate. Happiness consists not of having, but of being; not of possessing, but of enjoying. It is the warm glow of a heart at peace with itself. A martyr at the stake may have happiness that a king on his throne might envy. Man is the creator of his own happiness; it is the aroma of a life lived in harmony with high ideals. For what a man *has*, he may be dependent on others; what he *is*, rests with him alone. What he *obtains* in life is but acquisition; what he *attains* is growth. Happiness is the soul's joy in the possession of the intangible. Absolute, perfect, continuous happiness in life is impossible for the human. It would mean the consummation of attainments, the individual consciousness of a perfectly fulfilled destiny. Happiness is paradoxical because it may coexist with trial, sorrow and poverty. It is the gladness of the heart, rising superior to all conditions. . . . Man might possess everything tangible in the world and yet not be happy, for happiness is the satisfying of the soul, not of the mind or the body.

I am reminded of a vigorous man just past middle age who had some trouble that led to the amputation of one of his legs. But he took it cheerfully and very soon was back leading an active life again. Ten years later, the other leg had to be removed. I went to see him in the hospital. Inquiring my way to the right ward, I told the nurse in charge that I wanted to see Mr. Weiss.

"Oh, Mr. Weiss," she replied. "That man is the life of this hospital. He is the most joyful and enthusiastic patient we ever had. We just love him here."

She told me that a few days before, a drunken man—in a state of real inebriation—had come in carrying a big bunch of flowers, saying he was looking for a friend of his. The nurses didn't want to irritate the fellow if they could help it, so they let him walk through the ward, but he couldn't find his friend. Finally he said, "Okay, my friend isn't here. I will give my flowers to somebody else. I am going to give my flowers to the happiest person in this ward. I've got to go around and look at everyone." So he walked around staring at each face in turn. He said, "I never saw such a gloomy bunch of people." But then he came to Mr. Weiss. And through the fumes of alcohol his mind registered and he said, "You are a happy man. I can tell it. Here are the flowers. You are my friend."

As I talked with this man who had now lost both legs, I said, "They tell me you are the happiest, most enthusiastic man in the hospital. Where do you get all this happiness and enthusiasm? Let me in on the secret."

He pointed to the little table beside the bed. There was a Bible on it. "When I get to feeling a little low I read some of those wonderful words. Then I become lighthearted and life seems good." His secret was that he had learned one of the most difficult things there is to learn in life—one learned only by simplicity and by faith. He had learned to hold God's hand and trust Him. ". . . whoso trusteth in the Lord, happy is he" (Proverbs 16:20). The person who has faith in God's providence has a reserve of serenity deep inside even when things are very tough.

Upon leaving, as I shook hands with my inspiring friend, I said, "More power to you."

With a crushing handclasp and a big smile he responded, "The same to you—and we know where that power comes from, don't we?"

Here is a thought from Charles Dickens that may motivate us to develop joy and enthusiasm:

Cheerfulness and content are great beautifiers and are famous preservers of youthful looks.

The wise David Grayson suggests a source of joy that needs underscoring:

Joy of life seems to me to arise from a sense of being where one belongs. . . . All the discontented people I know are trying sedulously to be something they are not, to do something they cannot do. . . .

Contentment, and indeed usefulness, comes as the infallible result of great acceptances, great humilities—of not trying to make ourselves this or that (to conform to some dramatized version of ourselves), but of surrendering ourselves to the fulness of life—of letting life flow through us.

And the Bible reminds us of a basic way in which joy may be found:

But when the Holy Spirit controls our lives he will produce this kind of fruit in us: love, joy, peace, patience, kindness, goodness, faithfulness, gentleness and self-control. . . .

Galatians 5:22, 23 TLB

And when joy and enthusiasm are developed spiritually, we have a power greater than anything the world can do to us, as illustrated by this early Christian testimony quoted in Margaret Applegarth's book *Heirlooms*:

Pliny: I will banish thee.

Christian: Thou canst not, for the whole world is my Father's house.

Pliny: I will slay thee.

Christian: Thou canst not, for my life is hid with Christ in God.

Pliny: I will take away thy treasures.

Christian: Thou canst not, for my treasure is in heaven.

Pliny: I will drive thee away from men, and thou wilt have no friends left.

Christian: Thou canst not, for I have a Friend from whom thou canst
never separate me.

It must have been a person like that whom Henry Wadsworth
Longfellow had in mind:

> None but one can harm you,
> None but yourself who are your greatest foe;
> He that respects himself is safe from others:
> He wears a coat of mail that none can pierce.

Such persons as these had faith, the quality of faith that releases
power. They believed—wholeheartedly believed—and power came,
and with it often comes healing, as the following story by Frank
Kostyu illustrates:

> One day a poet and an artist were looking at a picture by
> the great French painter, Poussin, representing the healing of
> the two blind men at Jericho. Said the artist: "What seems to
> you the most remarkable thing about this picture?"
>
> "Well," the poet replied, "everything is excellently
> painted, the figure of Christ, the grouping of the individuals,
> the expressions on their faces."
>
> "But," said the artist, "look." And he pointed to the steps
> of a house shown in the corner of the canvas. "Do you see
> that discarded cane lying there?"
>
> "Yes, but what about it?"
>
> "Why," the artist replied, "on those steps the blind man sat
> with the cane in his hand, but when he heard Christ come he
> was so sure he would be healed that he let the cane lie there,
> and went to Christ as if he could already see."
>
> The Master made one demand on those who sought to be
> healed by him. It was belief. He understood the blocks that
> prevented the healing influence from working in the sick
> body or soul. So time and time again, he stressed the matter
> of belief. It was a primary prerequisite to being healed.

Actually joy is a lubricant for belief. It frees the mind and unlocks
the muscles. It puts us into rhythm. A truly joyful person is in God's

rhythm the same as the heavenly bodies are in His rhythmic processes.

Your internal system of blood and heart and organs constitutes a rhythm. And rhythm is another word for harmony, and harmony is another word for joy. Therefore, when you are joyful, you are in rhythm.

This is true of great athletes. In his book *The American Diamond*, perhaps the classic work on the game of baseball, Branch Rickey says that Honus Wagner was the greatest shortstop in baseball history. Mr. Rickey recalls how Wagner's whole body responded in such perfect rhythm that he scooped balls up from either side, he picked them out of the air, he reached for them wherever they were. And it is said that the reason for his vast ability was that he was a happy man. He loved the game and he loved life. Therefore, because of this joy, he was in harmony and he was in rhythm.

I once knew a tennis instructor who always emphasized the importance of joy and harmony in the game. Whenever he got a stiff pupil who did not have flexibility, his solution was to have him sing as he played.

One day he was instructing a girl who had real potential, but there was no harmonious flow in her game, despite her technical perfection. He asked her whether she knew "The Blue Danube Waltz." "As we play tennis," he said, "I want you to time your strokes to the rhythm of 'The Blue Danube Waltz.' "

As she played, she hummed the tune and her strokes began to increase in rhythm and symmetry. Afterward, her face aglow, she said, "I never felt the joy and thrill of this game before. For the first time in my life I feel I can master it." And similarly, joy and enthusiasm produce rhythm in the game of life, so that we can master it also.

I feel it should be pointed out that always in life, joy and enthusiasm are intermixed with pain, suffering, disappointment and other forms of trouble. But the joy and enthusiasm remain because we have the power through faith in God to see it through, to hang in there, to overcome. Annie Johnson Flint philosophizes factually:

WHAT GOD HATH PROMISED
God hath not promised
Skies always blue,

Flower-strewn pathways
All our lives through;
God hath not promised
Sun without rain,
Joy without sorrow,
Peace without pain.
But God hath promised
Strength for the day,
Rest for the labor,
Light for the way,
Grace for the trials,
Help from above,
Unfailing sympathy,
Undying love.

And Isaiah tells us in an immortal sentence (40:31) just how we keep going always with the power and the joy and the enthusiasm and the victory:

But they that wait upon the Lord shall renew their strength; they shall mount up with wings as eagles; they shall run, and not be weary; and they shall walk, and not faint.

Rufus M. Jones, a Quaker and a great spiritual leader, was one of the most thoughtful men of our time. He had experienced joy and sorrow. And he had spiritual power in full measure. Thinker that he was, he stated a profound fact:

The real test of a happy life is to see how much pain and loss and frustration can be endured and absorbed without spoiling the joy of it.

Life has been described in many ways; as a journey, a game, a battle, an adventure. But call it what you will, the one who lives must have the power. And that power working in his mind will give him the victory.

This book has as its purpose to help you, the reader, to grasp life now and know it in all its fullness. What better way to illustrate this than with a thought from that master of insight into human nature, William Shakespeare?

> There is a tide in the affairs of men,
> Which, taken at the flood, leads on to fortune;
> Omitted, all the voyage of their life
> Is bound in shallows and in miseries:
> And we must take the current when it serves,
> Or lose our ventures.
>
> *Julius Caesar*

More power to you. That phrase captions many a life story.

Some years ago I received a moving letter from a woman who told of learning to walk when it was assumed she could never do so. When I last heard from her she was in her eighties, still strengthened by the same positive faith described in her first letter:

I'm a little old lady in my late 60's and I would like to tell you and all the ones that have no faith that with the power of faith one can achieve miracles. I'm sorry I have no education and can't even spell right, but I'm going to try to relate to you my first great problem of my life and how I did draw on the power of faith.

I was born with dislocation of both my hips and doctors said I would never walk, but as I grew up and looked at others walk I said to myself, "Please, God, help me. I know You love me." I was six years old and my heart was broke and so one day I tryed to stand up between two chairs and down I would go but I didn't give up. Every day I'd speak to God and tryed again and again until I held myself up for a few seconds and I can't describe to you the joy in my heart being able to stand on my feet. I gave one scream to mama. "I'm up! I can walk!"

Then I went down again. I can't never forget the joy of my parents and when I tryed again my mother handed me the end of a broomstick while she held the other end and said, "Give one step forward with one foot and then another," and that is how my faith helped me to walk the duck walk, that's what the doctors call it but I have been so grateful ever since then.

Three years ago I had an accident and I broke my left ankle and was in the hospital and they took x-rays of my legs. Then the doctors came to me and said lady how did you walk? And I said God was my doctor and they said its a miracle you have no socketts and no joints on your hips how did you stand up? And memories came back to me and I have waited 60 years to find out that I have no socketts and no joints for I never knew why.

Then the doctors were afraid that with the accident and broken ankle and my age I would not walk again but God came to my rescue again and to the surprise of all I'm walking again, and still holding my job of taking care of four children of a widow mother while she works. I'm a widow too and had to work very hard to grow my children. My husband died with the spanish flu in 1919. I had two little girls and a son was born two months later. I scrubbed floors on my knees for 17 years and never was sick in my life I don't know what a headach is.

Another story, somewhat similar yet different in that the healing was mental rather than physical, has always appealed to me as one of the remarkable ways God works in human problems.

This is an incident from the experience of a man who became a newspaper editor. He was of French Canadian parentage and had been reared in Canada. He was born with a bad right leg; it was shriveled, atrophied and wouldn't bear any weight. So from infancy he wore a brace on this withered leg.

When he was a very little boy it didn't bother him overly much, but as he became older he realized that with a useless leg he couldn't compete. He could not run, play games, or climb trees like the other boys. So he got the impression that if he could not climb a tree, he could not climb the ladder of life. He began to develop an acute sense of being different—a sense of limitation and of inferiority. This misery went deeply into his mind, and he brooded over it and became gloomy and fearful about himself.

His father said to him, "Son, don't worry about your leg." And he told the boy that in the cathedral there was a big pile of crutches and braces left by people who had gone to the cathedral with maladies and disabilities and had been healed. He said, "Some day I am going to take you there, when I think you have matured enough so that you can believe; then we will pray and ask the Lord to heal you so you can leave your brace on the altar." The boy was impressed.

The great day came. Dressed in their Sunday best, father and son entered the great cathedral. The sun was streaming through the high stained-glass windows. Soft organ music reverberated through the aisles and arches. The little boy looked wonderingly around. When they arrived at the altar his father said, "Son, kneel and pray and ask the Lord to heal you."

The boy prayed most earnestly, prayed with faith and asked the Lord to heal him. He had a peaceful feeling inside. Then he lifted his eyes and looked at his father. He had always loved his father and had seen his face under many different circumstances. "But always," he said in later life, "will I remember the unearthly beauty that was on my father's face at that moment. There were tears in his eyes, and shining through was the joyous, exalted faith of the true believer."

Profoundly stirred, the boy stood up. But when he looked down, there was his withered leg, the same as before. Very depressed and despondent, he started down the aisle with his father, the old brace thumping along as usual. Then as they approached the huge door of the cathedral something incredible happened:

"I felt something tremendously warm in my heart. I seemed to feel something like a great hand pass across my head. I can feel to this day the lightness and yet the strength of that touch. Suddenly I was boundlessly happy. I cried, 'Father! You are right! I have been healed! I have been healed!'

"Young as I was, I knew what had happened. God had not taken the brace off my leg, but He had taken the brace off my mind."

From then on the withered leg had no power to dismay the boy. He grew in faith and confidence and went forward into a splendid career, the power with him all the way.

5

Faith and Successful Living

OCCASIONALLY I am asked what books have meant the most to me, and of course I could name many. But for present purposes I want to mention one. It contains a chapter "Enthusiasm," which I have read and reread for many years. The book is *How I Raised Myself From Failure to Success in Selling* by Frank Bettger, and I have mentioned it earlier in this book. While I am not a salesman, that chapter taught me an important truth about life generally. I would like to reprint the entire chapter here, but limitations of space prevent it. But I will give you in my own words the vital principle taught by Frank Bettger, for in my opinion it is important to successful living.

Bettger was a baseball player on a minor league team and, though technically a good player, he was fired for lack of enthusiasm. "Your heart just doesn't seem to be in the game, Frank," said the manager. "I'm sorry to let you go, but you're not alive enough."

Later, Bettger signed with another minor league club where he repeated the same desultory performance. A big league player who liked the young man and saw his possibilities said, "Frank, you have got to be more enthusiastic if you expect to get anywhere in baseball."

"But," complained Frank in despair, "I am just not enthusiastic. I'm not made that way. You can't go to a drugstore and buy a bottle of enthusiasm. If you haven't got it you just haven't got it."

"Oh, but you are so wrong, Frank. You can have enthusiasm by acting enthusiastic. We become what we act."

(The older player probably did not realize that he was teaching the younger man the famous "As If" principle of William James, mentioned earlier. James said that if you are a fearful person you can reeducate your mind to courage by deliberately acting *as if* you had courage. It was this same Professor James who said that a human being can alter his life by altering his attitude of mind.)

"So," said the older player, "start all over on a new club and from the first day act as if you were surcharged with enthusiasm." Frank Bettger was signed by New Haven. On his first day the temperature was over 90 degrees, but he threw the ball with such force it burned the hands of the players. He hit at everything and as a result got three hits in the game, and he ran the bases like a whirling dervish. The papers next day headlined "this ball of fire" and nicknamed him "Pep" Bettger. Soon a scout for the St. Louis Cardinals spotted him for his enthusiastic performance and he became their second baseman. Later he repeated the same "As If" principle of enthusiasm in the insurance business, becoming one of the top producers in the nation.

So, even if you feel tired and down—even sick—turn your thoughts to energy and act enthusiastic, until your subconscious mind takes over that concept. Your muscles will respond accordingly. There will be in you an amazing revitalization as you practice and keep on practicing the "As If" principle.

Among the many vital truths taught in the Bible is this one: "In him we live, and move, and have our being . . ." (Acts 17:28). Perhaps we can say it this way: *In Him we are alive and are energetic and enter fully into our being.* Sounds like being enthusiastic, does it not?

Nehemiah 8:10 says it well:

. . . for the joy of the Lord is your strength.

Act out in your own life the joy of the Lord— *live it, speak it, think it, be it*—and the joy of the Lord will indeed be your strength.

One of our great American founding fathers, Patrick Henry, whose fervent enthusiasm for liberty ignited the Revolution, was a wise and thoughtful man who knew how the Christian religion makes life better for everyone. When he made his last will and testament he wrote:

I have now disposed of all my property to my family. There is one thing more I wish I could give them, and that is the

Christian religion. If they had that, and I had not given them one shilling, they would have been rich; and if they had not that, and I had given them all the world, they would be poor.

No doubt Fatrick Henry had many things in mind when he expressed the desire to leave the Christian religion to his heirs. He wanted them to be aware of God and divine guidance, of the moral teachings of the Bible, and to accept Jesus Christ as their Savior. Judging by his own life and career, I am sure that he knew and valued the power of faith. He wanted it to be operative in the lives of his loved ones, as is suggested by the Bible verses which follow:

If thou canst believe, all things are possible to him that believeth.

Mark 9:23

What things soever ye desire, when ye pray, believe that ye receive them, and ye shall have them.

Mark 11:24

Whosoever shall say unto this mountain, Be thou removed, and be thou cast into the sea; and shall not doubt in his heart, but shall believe that those things which he saith shall come to pass; he shall have whatsoever he saith.

Mark 11:23

Be determined and confident. Study the book day and night. Make sure that you obey everything written in it. Then you will have good success. Be not afraid, for I your God am with you.

Joshua 1:7-9 paraphrased

. . . If ye have faith as a grain of mustard seed . . . nothing shall be impossible unto you.

Matthew 17:20

Dale Evans Rogers, entertainer and author, beloved by millions, points out that faith can make life successful. But, of greater value, it can make life abundant:

We rush through life so fast that we don't even know the flowers are there.

But it doesn't have to be like this. You can decide to do otherwise, to travel another way. This is *your* life. Choose ye this day. . . .

Now sooner or later in this life, like the man on the road to Jericho, we all discover that there are thieves lying in wait for us to rob us of our chance to really *live*. There are good values and bad values screaming for our money and/or our lives; there is God and the devil, and we will eventually travel with one or the other. You can't avoid it: you will have to choose between them. God cannot and will not do it for you. He gives you your years, your breath of life; you can use it either for Him or against Him.

Since I have come to know God and walk His way, the pressures and temptations that made my life so empty before I knew Him have disappeared completely. His power makes my life abundant instead of merely successful. He would do the same for you.

But faith can do even more. It can restore the lost beauty to a person and rehabilitate the misplaced or misused quality of one's nature and personality. Such a change occurred in the life story of a man who had read a book of mine. He was a very unhappy person, invariably dejected, his thinking cynical, negative and gloomy. He went on this way for several years. Then, for a while, I did not see him. Suddenly he wrote me a ten-page letter. I left it on my desk for quite a while before reading it; it looked so formidable. When finally I got into it I was amazed. Here was the lilting happy testimony of a man who at last had found himself and was telling me how happy he was. What had happened? That man had developed a five-fold program for himself, and through it had found the cure for his negativism and unhappiness. Here is how he described his program.

"*First*," he says, "I pray twenty-five times a day." If anybody will pray twenty-five times a day he will change the character of his thoughts, and so change his life.

Second, this man "soaks his mind" with Bible passages, imaging them as deeply penetrating his consciousness.

Third, he sits down with pen and paper and sees how many good thoughts he can write down about people he knows. He remarks that this was the toughest thing in the whole process. But if you think bad thoughts about people, you have a residue of unhappiness.

Next, he tells the Lord several times a day how much he loves Him.

Finally, the man tries to keep all sin out of his life.

The foregoing five-point spiritual-action program activated the power of faith to make this man over into a person of genuine joy and enthusiasm. As he himself described his new life-style, he was moving up from level to level and hoped ultimately to attain top-level life.

This man's experience reminded me of a wise insight of Pierre Teilhard de Chardin, in which he indicates that the ultimate in happiness is this moving upward to a higher state:

> Happiness has no existence nor value in itself, as an object which we can pursue and attain as such. It is no more than the sign, the effect, the reward (we might say) of appropriately directed action: a by-product, as Aldous Huxley says somewhere, of effort. Modern hedonism is wrong, accordingly, in suggesting that some sort of renewal of ourselves, no matter what form it takes, is all that is needed for happiness. Something more is required, for no change brings happiness unless the way in which it is effected involves an *ascent.*
>
> The happy man is therefore the man who, without any direct search for happiness, inevitably finds joy as an added bonus in the act of forging ahead and attaining the fullness and finality of his own self.

Faith of course is more than an intellectual belief in God. It is a closeness with God, a closeness to such degree that His loving and watchful care may be experienced in time of sorrow or crisis or danger. And this to a point where to call such care a matter of coincidence is to deny an obvious reality.

This is illustrated in a remarkable way by an event that happened in Shenkiu, in Central China's Honan Province, at the time of the Japanese invasion of China during World War II. The Japanese were approaching this city; they were very near—only two or three days away. The Chinese colonel came to the mission compound and told the pastor's wife that she had better leave, as he had received orders not to defend the city against the Japanese. The pastor, a medical missionary, had been taken to a hospital, himself ill. He was 115 miles away and would not return for perhaps a month. His wife was alone with a baby girl two months old and a two-year-old son.

An exodus from the city began. The elders of the church came and invited the missionary's wife to go with them to their villages. They were very kind and gracious people. But she had these two babies, and she knew that the village homes of these people were vermin-infested and full of germs. Western babies lacked the necessary immunity. There had been many deaths among missionaries' children exposed to conditions in the villages. Therefore, she was afraid to take her babies into those houses. So she remained in the city, alone, one American woman with two babies. The gatekeeper, her last protection, came and said that he, too, must leave. The poor woman was filled with fear. She was alone and unprotected, in bitter January weather, with the enemy approaching.

She went to the kitchen sink to fix a bottle for the baby. Her hands were cold. She shook so from fear that the bottle almost fell from her hands. Then she saw above the sink her Bible-text calendar. It was January 16, 1941, and beneath the date she read these words from Psalms 56:3: "What time I am afraid, I will trust in thee." She was astonished, but strangely comforted. All that night she kept her two little ones huddled close to her to keep them warm. She lay awake, listening to the wind rattle the paper windowpanes in the bamboo frames, praying to God, who, all the time she was afraid, would assuredly be with her. It was noon before she remembered to pull the page off the little daily calendar. The tenth verse of the Ninth Psalm proclaimed: "And they that know thy name will put their trust in thee: for thou, Lord, hast not forsaken them that seek thee." As she bowed her head over her noonday meal, she thanked God for those particular words at that moment.

When the following morning came, she realized that she was without food. All the stores were empty or closed, for there were no food supplies coming in from the countryside. All she had were the goats, but she did not know how to milk them. Once again, fear clutched at her. How would she feed the children? She pulled off the calendar page for January 17 and, believe it or not, under the date of January 18 were these words: "...I will nourish you, and your little ones" (Genesis 50:21). This modernly trained woman, schooled in the new thinking, asked herself, "Is this only a coincidence?"

Then came a rap at the door. It was a little Chinese woman, Mrs. Lee, a longtime neighbor. "We knew you would be hungry," she said, "and that you do not know how to milk the goats. So I have milked your goats. Here is milk for your children."

Presently another little woman came, holding a live chicken by the legs and also carrying some eggs. Once again the pastor's wife looked at the words, "I will nourish you, and your little ones."

That night her heart was full of hope. To the sound of shells bursting in the sky, she prayed that somehow God would spare the city and the gentle people whom these missionaries loved.

The next morning she rushed to the little calendar hanging on the nail and tore off the page. She read: "When I cry unto thee, then shall mine enemies turn back: this I know; for God is for me" (Psalms 56:9).

This time it seemed too much to believe! Surely a verse chosen by chance for a Scripture calendar couldn't be taken literally. And again fear clutched her. The Japanese army—what would they do with one lone, defenseless woman? She went through her husband's papers, destroying any that might be construed to incriminate her. She could hear the sound of gunfire coming closer and closer. She went to sleep that night fully dressed, prepared at any moment to meet the Japanese invaders.

She awoke in the early dawn expecting to hear rough shoes on the gravel, the sound of marching troops. But instead there was a deep quietness. Cautiously she went to the gate and watched as the streets began to fill, not with Japanese soldiers, but with townspeople coming back into the city. The colonel reappeared and said to her, "We don't understand it. The Japanese were headed for this city. They were going to take it. Suddenly they turned aside. We didn't defeat them. They just went another way and left our city unoccupied."

Was it coincidence? When you come right down to it, what *is* coincidence? Can it be an act of God in the midst of time, even modern time?

Faith, I believe, would so agree.
Many have found that reality in the glorious words of Isaiah 26:3:

> Thou wilt keep him in perfect peace, whose mind is stayed
> on thee: because he trusteth in thee.

Robert A. Russell writes:

> How did man get out of the Kingdom of God? How did he
> lose his place in it? By his negative thinking. How does he re-
> turn to it? How can he find expression in a Kingdom of Good
> only? By using the Mind of Christ, by allying his thoughts
> with the Divinity within him. If we are praying or speaking
> the word for some greater good, we know that Christ is
> speaking the word through us. "In all thy ways acknowledge
> Him, and He shall direct thy paths." "Delight thyself also in
> the Lord; and He shall give thee the desires of thine heart."

And Edna D. Cheney has expressed this faith in poetry:

THE LARGER PRAYER

At first I prayed for Light:
    Could I but see the way,
How gladly, swiftly would I walk
    To everlasting day!

And next I prayed for Strength:
    That I might tread the road
With firm, unfaltering feet, and win
    The heaven's serene abode.

And then I asked for Faith:
    Could I but trust my God,
I'd live enfolded in His peace,
    Though foes were all abroad.

But now I pray for Love:
    Deep love to God and man,

A living love that will not fail,
However dark His plan.

And Light and Strength and Faith
Are opening everywhere;
God only waited for me, till
I prayed the larger prayer.

According to Fulton Oursler, men like Washington, who said, "The event is in the hands of God," and Adams and Lincoln had no trouble in separating coincidence from the mighty acts of God operating in human affairs:

"It is impossible to rightfully govern the world without God and the Bible," said George Washington, and John Adams called it "the best book in the world," while Lincoln said, ". . . Take all of this book upon reason that you can and the balance by faith and you will live and die a better man."

The Greatest Book Ever Written

I once knew a scientist who was also a great spiritual leader. Dr. Albert E. Cliffe taught every Sunday the largest Bible class in Canada. I like Dr. Cliffe's reminder that we have an intelligent God who wants us to be happy and so helps us through our faith:

God's intelligence is available to your intelligence for use, for guidance and inspiration. He wants you to be a happy, successful, healthy person, and He is ever waiting for you to use His power through Jesus Christ.

Let Go and Let God

Perhaps two of the most powerful forces in this life, which affect persons for either good or bad, are faith and fear. Indeed, the only force more powerful than fear is faith. And faith can overcome fear.

Positive faith is closely associated with common sense. Tackle a fear-centered situation with sound reason and you gain the courage to deal with it effectively.

A friend had a long bout with a disease. He attacked his illness in his usual businesslike manner. He had it—that was that—and he proceeded to fit the treatments into his daily schedule. He went on with his business, never showing any emotion. I asked him, "At any time during this experience were you afraid?"

"Yes," he replied, "there was one time when I was afraid. That was when my temperature stayed at 104 degrees for three days. The thought crossed my mind that maybe I wasn't going to make it. But I was afraid only temporarily. I just began to apply common sense, and as I did so the fever went down. All the common sense I had told me that the doctors on this case were confident that they were doing the right thing." And he added, "Beyond that, I was in good hands. When I board a plane I'm not afraid. I know the equipment is good. I know the plane has been well serviced, that the pilots and engineers know their business. I don't sit there being afraid. I apply common sense to it. I am in a scientific universe."

"Well," I commented, "you're one man who doesn't seem to have fear in the slightest degree."

"Why should I?" he replied, "I gave my mind to Jesus Christ. He freed me of fear. And when you do that you don't need to be afraid of anything."

"For God hath not given us the spirit of fear; but of power, and of love, and of a sound mind" (2 Timothy 1:7). Such is the positive faith that gave courage to this man.

Sometimes it is necessary to do battle with your fear and kill it. There are times when no lesser method will suffice. Emerson in a famous statement said, "Do the thing you fear and the death of fear is certain."

Somewhere (if I knew the source, I would gladly acknowledge it), I read a thrilling story about a man in the South African gold fields by the name of Courteney. He had started as a working miner and eventually owned a gold mine. As he was working his way up he was tough as nails, but after he acquired the gold mine he became rich and fat and soft.

One day he went down into the mine and there came a rumbling in the earth that became an underground cataclysm. The miners ran. They were lithe and lean and got away. But he was fat and slow and was trapped by falling rock. All the lights went out. Fortunately, there was a piece of metal above his head that shored up the rocks directly above him, giving him space enough to stand erect with about five inches clearance. But the rocks grating and settling all around him closed him in with just enough room to move his elbows a bit. Dust filled the air. He managed to tear off a piece of his shirt and put it over his nose to avoid suffocation.

He realized his predicament well: he was many feet beneath the surface of the earth, entirely alone, entombed by rocks. That old devil, claustrophobia, seized him. He wanted to shriek and scream. But his mind told him it would be of no avail and that he must preserve his strength. He had just enough air to sustain life for a while.

At length he heard in the silence the tap of metal on stone and knew that relief was coming. By a herculean effort of prayer and faith he controlled himself until the rescue workers reached him. Finally came cool, sweet air and he was taken out to safety.

But that night in bed it suddenly seemed as though the darkness was closing in on him again; it was as if the bedclothes were rocks falling all around him. With a cry of terror he threw back the covers, leaped from the bed and ran outside. He breathed the fresh air and looked up at the stars and the moon. The terror subsided. But he sat up the remainder of the night.

Night after night he tried to sleep, but always the terror would come over him. He knew his faith must be deepened. He prayed and asked the Lord how to handle his problem.

One day he told his friends that he was going to be gone for a little while—that he was going "to kill a devil." He went to the mine shaft and told the man who ran the lift to take him down to the fourteenth level. The man refused. "Mr. Courteney, I can't take you to the fourteenth level. It's not shored up properly down there. We haven't worked it for a long time. It's very dangerous. I can't take you down, sir."

"Look, my friend," said Courteney, "I own this mine. Take me down to the fourteenth level." Reluctantly, the man took him down. Then Courteney said, "Now take the lift up and leave me here."

The darkness crept around him and with it came the terror. He started walking down a tunnel. He could hear water dripping. He knew that this tunnel was shored up with very old timbers that had been there for many years. He heard a rumble in the earth. His heart beat faster. Cold sweat came upon his face. Terror seized him. But he prayed, "Lord, Lord, help me. I must kill this devil of fear or I will die." He stayed there in the darkness of the mine, affirming faith until the devil lay dead. Then he signaled for the lift and was taken up. He said to the lift operator, "There's a dead devil down below." He walked out into peace, in control of himself.

Kill a devil, the devil of fear, the devil that drives you and haunts you all your life. There has to come a time when your faith becomes so deep and positive that you can kill that fear, leaving it dead, finished. Only faith can kill fear. ". . . Take heart, it is I; have no fear" (Matthew 14:27 RSV). And when a person develops power over fear, then joy and enthusiasm will be boundless. And it is faith that leads to that highly desirable mental condition.

My wife and I had lunch one cold day in a charming old restaurant in Bath, England; afterward we sat before an open fire for a while in a little parlor where on the wall was this framed ancient prayer:

> I arise today
>   in the might of Heaven
>   brightness of the sun
> whiteness of the snow
> splendour of fire
>   I arise today
> in the Might of God for my piloting
>   Wisdom of God for my guidance
> Eye of God for my foresight
> Ear of God for my hearing
>   I evoke therefore all these forces:
> against every fierce merciless force that may
> come upon my body and soul;
> against incantations of false prophets;
> against false laws of heresy;
> against black laws of paganism;
> against deceit of idolatry;
> against spells of woman, smiths, and druids;
> against all knowledge that is forbidden the human soul.
> against poison, against burning
> against drowning, against wounding,
> that there may come to me a multitude of rewards.

> Christ with me, Christ before me,
> Christ behind me, Christ in me,
> Christ under me, Christ over me.

Think of it: You can arise today in the might of Heaven, against all sorrow, defeat, against all your fears. So, when plagued by anxiety, worry, apprehension or fear, affirm that God is good, affirm that God loves you. Affirm that God is taking care of you. And the forces of fear will be driven off. Positive faith will increase your courage always.

Having faith, we can walk through this world with urbanity and courage, living successfully and with joy and enthusiasm every day all the way. The famous psychiatrist, Dr. Carl G. Jung, considered faith important to mental and physical well-being:

> Among all my patients in the second half of life—that is to say, over thirty-five, there has not been one whose problem in the last resort was not that of finding a religious outlook on life. It is safe to say that every one of them fell ill because he had lost that which the living religious of every age have given to their followers, and none of them has been really healed who did not regain his religious outlook.

And Archbishop William Temple agrees:

> The causes of health, as the causes of sickness, are very many, but among the forces which will tend to keep us in health will be a faith which is extended to a real expectation of God's goodness in every department of our being. That will bring us either actual health or a greater power of triumphing over ill-health, and either of these is a great blessing. Moreover, when we triumph in the way that I have described over ill-health, the result is, in fact, that our health is somewhat better than if we were merely lying passive in the grip of our disease, because owing to the exaltation of mind there is a real access of vitality which tends to combat the disease itself.

The healing power of faith is illustrated by one of America's greatest preachers, Dr. Charles L. Allen, who tells of a troubled man who came to him for help and to whom he gave a healing "prescription":

If you could look at this man who came to see me, you would think that he never had had a worry in his life.

I asked him his trouble; it was that he could not sleep at night. He told me he had not had a full night's sleep in six months.

We continued talking, and finally he said, "I have everything a man should want in life, but I am just plain scared and I do not know why I am scared."

I took a sheet of paper and wrote across the top of it these words: "HE LEADETH ME BESIDE THE STILL WATERS." I handed him the sheet of paper and told him to put it in his pocket and before he went to bed that night to write down under the quotation everything he thought it meant and whatever related thoughts it brought to mind. Then he was to put the paper in his dresser drawer. The following night he was to take out what he had written, read it over, and add whatever additional thoughts had come to him. He was to keep that up every night for a week and then come back to see me.

I wanted to saturate his mind completely with that one thought. I know that it is utterly impossible to keep fear and thoughts of "still waters" in a mind at the same time. Any good fisherman can testify to that. That is the reason that fishing is such a great medicine for so many people.

There is no nerve medicine on this earth to be compared with still waters; when we create those clear, cool, still waters on the screen of our imagination, it is wonder-working. As Longfellow put it, "Sit in revery, and watch the changing color of the waves that break upon the idle seashore of the mind."

Another bit of wisdom is to live a day at a time. Robert J. Burdette says it well:

There are two days in the week upon which and about which I never worry—two carefree days kept sacredly free from fear and apprehension.

One of these days is yesterday. Yesterday, with its cares and frets and all its pains and aches, all its faults, its mistakes and blunders, has passed forever beyond my recall.

It was mine.

It is God's.

And the other day that I do not worry about is tomorrow. Tomorrow, with all its possible adversities, its burdens, its perils, its large promise and poor performance, its failures and mistakes, is as far beyond my mastery as its dead sister, yesterday.

Tomorrow is God's day.

It will be mine.

There is left for myself, then, but one day in the week— today. Any woman can carry the burdens of just one day. Any man can resist the temptations of today.

It is only when we add the burdens of those two awful eternities, yesterday and tomorrow, that we break down.

The literature on successful living in America is vast and varied, for Americans have historically been attracted by the idea of doing the best they can with their lives. So here are eight steps to success in life by the great early American showman, P. T. Barnum:

1. Engage in a business for which you have a talent.
2. Secure a suitable locality for your business.
3. Stick to your business. Do not assume that just because you are a success in one field that you can be so in any.
4. Be economical; not parsimonious, nor stingy, but never go into debt.
5. Be systematic. No man can succeed in business who neglects the strict observance of system in his business.
6. Advertise. Have a good article and make it known in some way to the public that you have such a thing for sale.
7. Be charitable. It always pays a businessman to perform acts of benevolence.

8. Be honest. Honesty is the best policy. A man who lacks honesty will soon lack customers for his goods.

The early American preacher Jonathan Edwards comes up with similar advice:

> Resolved: To live with all my might while I do live.
> Resolved: Never to lose one moment of time, but improve it in the most profitable way I possibly can.
> Resolved: Never to do anything which I should despise or think meanly of in another.
> Resolved: Never to do anything out of revenge.
> Resolved: Never to do anything which I should be afraid to do if it were the last hour of my life.

And William James joins the chorus of wisdom for successful living:

> We forget that every good that is worth possessing must be paid for in strokes of daily effort. We postpone and postpone until these smiling possibilities are dead. By neglecting the necessary concrete labor, by sparing ourselves the little daily tax, we are positively digging the graves of our higher possibilities.

I like the thought expressed by Winfred Rhoades that what we become within ourselves is the true success. And to become that, faith is a vital ingredient:

> Life's supreme adventure is the adventure of living. Life's greatest achievement is the continual remaking of yourself so that at last you do know how to live.
> The man who is set for the building up of a self he can live with in some kind of comfort and with the hope of continued improvement chooses deliberately what he will let himself think and feel, thoughts of admiration and high desire, emotions that are courageous and inspiring. It is by these that we grow into more abundant and truer life, a more harmonious inner state and a more stalwart personality.

6
The Value of a Positive Attitude

WILLIAM ARTHUR WARD, creator of many wise sayings, reminds us that:

A cloudy day is no match for a sunny disposition.

It is also true that a positive attitude is a match for all the gloom and depression that affects so many these days. It is almost magical how a sunny disposition and joyfully positive attitude chases gloom away.

Frank Kostyu says:

In town I stopped to talk to a business friend. It was a cold, dreary day and, as might be expected, the conversation opened with some remarks about the weather.

"It certainly is a gloomy day," I said.

Then he told me an interesting thing that had happened to him on just such a dismal day. He left the house one morning dreading to go to his place of business. From the house next door, his friendly neighbor called, "Hello, neighbor! It's a great day!"

My friend looked up, observed that many trees were still in full autumn color. The air was clean to breathe.

"Yes," he answered, a little more cheerfully, "it is a great day."

He straightened his shoulders, walked down to the corner barber shop and said to the boys, "It is a great day!"

They smiled back, "It sure is!"

When he arrived at his store, he spoke to his clerks. "It's a great day!" They all looked up and smiled.

Wherever he went that day he radiated the happy spirit, and when he arrived home in the evening he said to his wife, "This has indeed been a great day. It looked dismal at the beginning, but everything seemed to turn for the better and the whole day was bright." His wife reflected his spirit. She, too, seemed happy.

A cheerful word changed the whole day.

Charles Kingsley believed that a sunny disposition has much to do with a successful career:

The men I have seen succeed have always been cheerful and hopeful, who went about their business with a smile on their faces, and took the changes and chances of this mortal life like men . . . If you wish to be miserable, you must think about yourself; about what you want, what you like, what respect people ought to pay you, what people think of you, and then to you nothing will be pure. You will spoil everything you touch; you will make sin and misery out of everything God sends you; you can be as wretched as you choose.

"But," you may say, "it's not always easy to have a positive and sunny attitude." To which we suggest the following for consideration:

I can do all things through Christ which strengtheneth me.
                                                        Philippians 4:13

And Ella Wheeler Wilcox gives us some wise counsel in her poem "Optimism":

Talk happiness. The world is sad enough
Without your woes. No path is wholly rough;
Look for the places that are smooth and clear,
And speak of those, to rest the weary ear

Of Earth, so hurt by one continuous strain
Of human discontent and grief and pain.

Talk faith. The world is better off without
Your uttered ignorance and morbid doubt.
If you have faith in God, or man, or self,
Say so. If not, push back upon the shelf
Of silence all your thoughts, till faith shall come;
No one will grieve because your lips are dumb.

Talk health. The dreary, never-changing tale
Of mortal maladies is worn and stale.
You cannot charm, or interest, or please
By harping on that minor chord, disease.
Say you are well, or all is well with you,
And God shall hear your words and make them true.

While we are considering the joy of a positive attitude, it may also be well to think of the contrary attitude of unhappiness. The famous writer and psychologist William James says:

The attitude of unhappiness is not only painful, it is also mean and ugly.

What can be more base and unworthy than the pining, puling, mumping mood, no matter by what outward ills it may have been engendered?

What is more injurious to others?

What less helpful as a way out of difficulty?

It but fastens and perpetuates the trouble which occasioned it, and increases the total evil of the situation.

This brings to mind the old man I heard about who was a guest on a television show with a famous emcee. It seems that this man was on the program on his ninetieth birthday because he was noted for his physical well-being and his joyful spirit. He was a marvelous raconteur and kept everyone entertained by his stories, his humorous quips and wise remarks. He really stole the show. But the emcee didn't mind; in fact, he was enjoying his guest immensely. Finally he said, "Our time is just about up, but one more question. You seem a genuinely happy man. How did you get that way?"

"Sure, I'm happy," replied the old gentleman. "You see, it's this way. Every morning when I wake up I have two choices: one—to be unhappy, or two—to be happy. And since I'm not dumb, I just choose to be happy. It's as plain as the nose on your face."

And so it is, really, but perhaps we let life awe us, actually persuading us that living is so complex and difficult that we are even under the control of circumstances; whereas actually it can be just the other way around. As Daniel C. Steere says:

> Life is very manageable. It is intended to be. Life is exciting, and positive, and rewarding.
>
> Life is the most marvelous tool God has created for you. Everything on earth has been put here at man's disposal. God intends for you to use life. He wants you to take advantage of all the things He has put here, and to use them as resources and opportunities.
>
> There are two crucial concepts for improving self-confidence. The first is: Who you are will always be consistent with who you think you are. The second is that you are an underachiever! There are enough buried reserves of capability and talent for you to be anyone you want to be.
>
> Add to those basic concepts of yourself a third basic truth. This fact is about life:
>
> Most people have to overcome their awe of life before they can master it!

The famous writer Sydney Smith, back in the 1700s, stated the simple principle of choice put forward by the elderly man on the television show. He said, adding a warning:

> When you arise in the morning, form a resolution to make the day a happy one to a fellow-creature.
>
> Never give way to melancholy; resist it steadily, for the habit will encroach.

A positive attitude that is joyful and enthusiastic will, if sincerely long held, produce joyful, enthusiastic and positive results in our lives.

Dr. Albert E. Cliffe wrote a great and inspiring book called *Let Go and Let God*, in which he says:

> "He that will love life, and see good days ... let him es-chew evil, and do good."
>
> 1 Peter 3:10–11

If we hold such negative thoughts until they dominate our minds, if we look for sin and sickness in everyone, we will certainly find it.

Every day can be a blue day to you, every night just another night of misery; you produce in your daily life these very things by constantly impressing wrong ideas upon your mind. Every person living on this earth is as he is because of the pattern of his past thinking, and if your life has been unhappy up to now, then it is time for you to change your ideas and begin to practice a Christianity that will radiate happy living into your experiences.

Many of you enjoyed, no doubt, during the last summer a wonderful vacation, going to new places, seeing new areas of nature, meeting different people all living very different lives from your own. You came back with a thoroughly different picture of life from that which you had before. You came home refreshed, after being absent for some time from your daily toil, your daily worries, the people who annoyed you. Oh, how much you enjoyed the change. You lived happily during your vacation.

Was it a miserable world to you then? Did you not enjoy every minute of it? Did you not love the beauties of the sea, the forest, the countryside, the lake shore? Was it a hell on earth to you or was it a picture of God's perfection? You had a complete change of scene and peace of mind. In those few weeks you changed the pattern of your thinking, and what did you find? In the beauties of nature you found God and you found a heaven on earth. You loved life while on your vacation, didn't you? Then why is it not possible to enjoy this happy living three hundred and sixty-five days a year?

The Bible says, "He that will love life and see good days," and this tells you very definitely that the Master, Jesus Christ, knows all about life, knows all about the good in life, all about good living, and He wants you as a child of His Father, to share that good life, to be happy with Him right now.

Can you imagine the Master, Jesus, as a sad-faced, weary, miserable-looking person, a man without personality, a negative individual thinking only of the miseries of life? Would such a man have brought Lazarus back from his eternal home to continue on such an earth if it were a place of misery? It isn't common sense.

You can make your life a happy one if first of all you will forget and forgive the past, if you will learn to live one day at a time, believing that a radiant future is yours.

Fears and diseases will follow you no more when you learn from the depths of your heart how to let go the evils of your life and let God take care of you.

There is a simple technique for living the Christian life. First of all you must believe in and accept the teachings of the Master. You must read about Him every day in the Gospels. You must make an appointment with Him every day to talk to Him. Through this simple faith you will demonstrate a life of overflowing abundance and overwhelming happiness. You will learn how to put yourself last in your life, and your fellowmen before yourself. You will then have a most powerful mental attitude towards life. This is faith, and the Bible is full of stories of what faith has done for others and what faith in a living vibrant Christ will do for you. Nothing in this world will be impossible to you.

What about the promise, "What things soever ye desire, when ye pray, believe that ye receive them, and ye shall have them"? What a marvelous promise this is, and how true you can prove it to be.

Stanley Jones says that it is much more fun being a Christian than going to the devil; one feeds a life, the other satisfies an impulse. One ends in a mess, the other in the joy of living.

Many things will happen to you when you take Jesus Christ as your guide to happiness. Many little coincidences will take place in your daily life which you had previously looked upon as good luck. But they are all part of that divine plan, for the world is created by a God who runs it on laws, and when you live up to those laws, then you *let go and let God*. The joy of living becomes a daily coincidence with you. . . .

A businessman came to see me some time ago who had failed in business. While he seemed to have good ideas, he did not have enough working capital. After discussing his life with me, we discovered he was filled with criticism and resentment of former employers and his life was dominated by these resentments. He had to ask forgiveness of his employers. He had to ask forgiveness of God. He had to seek peace and follow it; he had to surrender his life to Christ. Then he gained his answer. Several offers of capital came to him from sources he had never known before, and the more he practiced living one day at a time, the more he forgot that wicked past, and the more successful he became.

Do you believe that God wants you to live a miserable life? Do you believe that He wants you to have worries, anxieties and sicknesses? That is not the teaching of the New Testament. He wants you to be happy and to radiate that happiness.

Many people want to be happy but do not know how. They take their happiness from the material things of life; but do you often see happy faces leaving a movie or cocktail bar? Not really happy faces.

Then we have that type of Christian so proud to tell you how long he has been saved, who thinks it a crime to smile in church. I often wonder why so many Christians frown so much in their daily lives and in their jobs. They don't realize that it takes twenty-seven face muscles to form a frown, and only eight to make a smile. This kind of Christian naturally overworks his face.

The teachings of Jesus make us happy, radiant, joyful, successful. Jesus makes you glad; He makes you sing. . . .

Your guide to happiness is the Christ—His way of life.

Do you want it? There is a price to be paid. You must surrender your whole self to God through Jesus Christ. Pray for it, act on it, believe it, and you will begin at once to feel His power in you. Plant this idea firmly in your mind, affirm it every day, strive for it. Try to make yourself worthy of being a temple for His Spirit. . . . There is not a soul upon earth who cannot make his or her life a marvelous thing, a tremendous experience.

Let go those things in life which have kept you from happiness, *and let God.*

The foregoing reminds me of a charming one-liner by Janet Lane:

Of all the things you wear, your expression is the most important.

And I also like these verses by G. J. Russell, a sound, commonsense philosopher:

IT MIGHT HAVE BEEN WORSE
Sometimes I pause and sadly think
    Of the things that might have been,
Of the golden chances I let slip by,
    And which never returned again.

Think of the joys that might have been mine;
    The prizes I almost won,
The goals I missed by a mere hair's breadth;
    And the things I might have done.

It fills me with gloom when I ponder thus,
    Till I look on the other side,
How I might have been completely engulfed
    By misfortune's surging tide.

The unknown dangers lurking about,
    Which I passed safely through
The evils and sorrows that I've been spared
    Pass plainly now in review.

> So when I am downcast and feeling sad,
> I repeat over and over again,
> Things are far from being as bad
> As they easily might have been.

Robert Louis Stevenson's philosophy also represents a positive attitude:

> As yesterday is history, and tomorrow may never come, I have resolved from this day on, I will do all the business I can honestly, have all the fun I can reasonably, do all the good I can willingly, and save my digestion by thinking pleasantly.

The famed religious leader, John Wesley, had, it would seem, a proper self-appraisal of his relationship to the universe:

> He who governed the world before I was born shall take care of it likewise when I am dead. My part is to improve the present moment.

We must never lose sight of the fact that the important thing is not what happens to you but, rather, your attitude toward what happens. A friend once gave me a carved-wood plaque which I have on my wall. It reads in raised letters, ATTITUDES ARE MORE IMPORTANT THAN FACTS.

When this was first given to me I thanked my friend but disagreed with the statement. "Nothing," I said, "can be more important than a fact, for a fact is a fact and that is that."

"Nothing," he replied, "is more important than your attitude toward the fact."

He illustrated his point this way: Here is a big, hard fact. And to deal with this fact are two men, both of equal mentality, equal education, equal ability. One man approaches the fact and is awed by it. "What a huge fact," he says. "This fact is really overwhelming and tough." And as he thinks and talks the fact gets bigger and the man smaller. The result is that he is defeated by the fact.

The second man approaches the same fact and recognizes its complexity; he does not minimize it. But he is not only a realist about the difficulty inherent in the fact, he is a positive thinker and takes a positive attitude toward the fact and—what is more important—toward himself also. He reasons, "This is indeed a tough fact, but I am tougher than the fact. I'm bigger than this fact. I have the know-how or I know how to get the know-how, and with God's help I can handle this situation"—which he proceeds to do and successfully deals with the fact. Because of his attitude he demonstrates that attitudes are indeed more important than facts.

John Homer Miller agrees with this positive point of view:

COLORS

Your living is determined not so much by what life brings to you as by the attitude you bring to life; not so much by what happens to you as by the way your mind looks at what happens. Circumstances and situations do color life, but you have been given the mind to choose what the color shall be.

Even an attitude toward dark nights and storms, even toward despair, can become joyful, John Kendrick Bangs tells us:

> I never knew a night so black
> Light failed to follow on its track.
> I never knew a storm so gray
> It failed to have its clearing day.
> I never knew such bleak despair
> That there was not a rift, somewhere.
> I never knew an hour so drear
> Love could not fill it full of cheer!

And I like that poem by Robert E. Farley called "Thinking Happiness," which tells how the happiness attitude results in joy and enthusiasm:

> Think of the things that make you happy,
> Not the things that make you sad;
> Think of the fine and true in mankind,
> Not its sordid side and bad;
> Think of the blessings that surround you,

> Not the ones that are denied;
> Think of the virtues of your friendships,
> Not the weak and faulty side;
>
> Think of the gains you've made in business,
> Not the losses you've incurred;
> Think of the good of you that's spoken,
> Not some cruel, hostile word;
> Think of the days of health and pleasure,
> Not the days of woe and pain;
> Think of the days alive with sunshine,
> Not the dismal days of rain;
>
> Think of the hopes that lie before you,
> Not the waste that lies behind;
> Think of the treasures you have gathered,
> Not the ones you've failed to find;
> Think of the service you may render,
> Not of serving self alone;
> Think of the happiness of others,
> And in this you'll find your own!

The philosopher Arthur Schopenhauer points out that joy from within is the best form of happiness and that our own personal world is determined by how we look at it, or our attitude toward it:

> The happiness which we receive from ourselves is greater than that which we obtain from our surroundings. . . . The world in which a man lives shapes itself chiefly by the way in which he looks at it.

The development of a positive attitude requires effort and may not come easily. We are born with a positive attitude. At least, I do not believe I ever saw a negative baby. But that same child may be born into a negative family climate. And being absorbent—a sponge of prevailing attitudes, so to speak—the child soon takes on the mental atmosphere prevalent in the family. When, later as a young person, the child now wants to become a positive thinker, he or she must begin a mental reeducation process which can be long and difficult, even painful, for old thought habits die hard. To achieve a new and positive attitude may indeed, perhaps definitely will, require practice, discipline and continuous vigilance to avoid slipping back into the old negative thought pattern.

Perhaps one might work out for oneself a procedure of thought practice such as that which Sybil F. Partridge employed:

JUST FOR TODAY

Just for today I will be happy.

This assumes that what Abraham Lincoln said is true, that "most folks are about as happy as they make up their minds to be." Happiness is from within; it is not a matter of externals.

Just for today I will try to adjust myself to what is, and not try to adjust everything to my own desires.

I will take my family, my business and my luck as they come and fit myself to them.

Just for today I will take care of my body.

I will exercise it, care for it, nourish it, not abuse it nor neglect it, so that it will be a perfect machine for my bidding.

Just for today I will try to strengthen my mind.

I will learn something useful. I will not be a mental loafer. I will read something that requires effort, thought and concentration.

Just for today I will exercise my soul in three ways.

I will do somebody a good turn and not get found out. I will do at least two things I don't want to do, as William James suggests, just for exercise.

Just for today I will be agreeable.

I will look as well as I can, dress as becomingly as possible, talk low, act courteously, be liberal with praise, criticize not at all, nor find fault with anything and not try to regulate nor improve anyone.

Just for today I will try to live through this day only.

Not to tackle my whole life problem at once. I can do things for twelve hours that would appall me if I had to keep them up for a lifetime.

Just for today I will have a program.

I will write down what I expect to do every hour. I may not follow it exactly, but I will have it. It will eliminate two pests, hurry and indecision.

Just for today I will have a quiet half-hour all by myself and relax.

In this half-hour sometimes I will think of God, so as to get a little more perspective into my life.

Just for today I will be unafraid.

Especially I will not be afraid to be happy, to enjoy what is beautiful, to love, and to believe that those I love, love me.

Frank Bettger went through the attitude reeducation process, which he describes to a degree, at least, in the following:

Soon after I started out to sell, I discovered that a worried, sour expression brought results that were just about infallible—an unwelcome audience and failure.

It didn't take me long to realize that I had a serious handicap to overcome. I knew it wasn't going to be easy to change that worried expression on my face left by so many years of hardship. It meant complete change in my outlook on life. Here is the method I tried. It began to show results *immediately* in my home, socially, and in business.

Each morning during a fifteen-minute bath and vigorous rubdown, I determined to cultivate a big, happy smile, just for that fifteen minutes. I soon discovered, however, that it couldn't be an insincere, commercialized smile, developed just for the purpose of putting dollars in my pocket. It had to be an honest-to-goodness smile from down deep inside, an outward expression of happiness from within!

No, it wasn't easy at first. Time and again I found myself during that fifteen-minute workout thinking thoughts of doubt, fear, and worry. Result? The old worried face again! A smile and worry simply won't mix, so once again I'd force the smile. Back came cheerful, optimistic thoughts.

Although I didn't realize it until later, this experience seems to substantiate the theory of the great philosopher and teacher, Professor William James of Harvard: "Action *seems* to follow feeling, but really action and feeling go together; and by regulating the action, which is under the more direct control of the will, we can indirectly regulate the feeling, which is not."

Let's see how starting off with a good fifteen-minute workout of the smile muscles helped me during the day. Before entering a man's office I would pause for an instant and think of the many things I had to be thankful for, work up a great big, honest-to-goodness smile, and then enter the room with the smile just vanishing from my face. It was easy then to turn on a big, happy smile. Seldom did it fail to get the same kind of smile in return from the person I met on the inside. When Miss Secretary went in to the boss and announced me I feel sure she reflected some part of the smiles we'd exchanged in the outer office, for she would usually come back still wearing that smile.

Let's assume for a moment that I had gone in looking worried, or forcing one of those rubber-band smiles—you know, the kind that snaps right back—don't you think that secretary's expression would have practically told her boss *not* to see me? Then walking into the boss's office, it was natural for me to give him a happy smile as I said: "Mr. Livingston! Good morning!"

That the positive attitude reeducation process is important in leading to joy and enthusiasm is indicated by Dr. Albert E. Cliffe:

Negative thinking will always lead to failure and nervous prostration; but positive faith—positive thinking—will lead you towards happy, healthy and abundant living.

Finally, there are always those who dolefully say, "It can't be done." These negativists and pessimists probably want others to fail, perhaps to justify their own deficiencies. It is undoubtedly wiser to listen to creative people like Edgar A. Guest who say that it *can* be done. They are the positive people who help others to achieve the best in life through joy and enthusiasm.

IT COULDN'T BE DONE

Somebody said that it couldn't be done,
    But he with a chuckle replied
That "maybe it couldn't," but he would be one
    Who wouldn't say so till he'd tried.
So he buckled right in with the trace of a grin
    On his face. If he worried he hid it.
He started to sing as he tackled the thing
    That couldn't be done, and he did it.

Somebody scoffed: "Oh, you'll never do that;
    At least no one ever has done it";
But he took off his coat and he took off his hat,
    And the first thing we knew he'd begun it.
With a lift of his chin and a bit of a grin,
    Without any doubting or quiddit,
He started to sing as he tackled the thing
    That couldn't be done, and he did it.

There are thousands to tell you it cannot be done,
    There are thousands to prophesy failure;
There are thousands to point out to you, one by one,
    The dangers that wait to assail you.
But just buckle in with a bit of a grin,
    Just take off your coat and go to it;
Just start to sing as you tackle the thing
    That "cannot be done," and you'll do it.

                             EDGAR A. GUEST

7

Life With a Spiritual Upthrust

WITH GOOD REASON we have been encouraged to pray and know the Bible, for in this manner we become conditioned with a *spiritual upthrust*. Joy, enthusiasm and vitality of spirit result from a mounting tide of spiritual power within the personality.

Recently a man whom I have known for many years took me to his club for lunch. The members of the club sat at a huge round table and although my host had told me that he wanted me to entertain the group, I had no chance to do so, for my host was the center of a sparkling, vivacious and positively fascinating conversation. I studied him with amazement, for I remember the time, years before, when his father came to me and said, "What can I do with my son? He fails at everything he touches. I think he is intelligent. He has had a good education. But he is so dull and apathetic and spiritually down that I despair of him." Had my friend's father been alive and at the luncheon, I'm sure he would have looked with astonishment at his son.

Naturally I wanted to know the secret, so later I asked him.

"There is no secret," he said. "All I did was to start using that idea of taking God as your partner. Now, every day of my life I read the New Testament; it is filled to overflowing with life."

The Bible is filled with life. Take a concordance and look up the words that are mentioned most often in the Bible. You will find that they are *life, love* and *faith*. "In him was life . . . (John 1:4). The idea is that if you really center your life in Christ, the deadness, the gloom, the apprehension, the weariness, the disgust, the tiredness will fall away.

How does one become filled with such joyous vitality? Everybody wants this. How does one acquire it?

It is the old phenomenon of a human being making actual contact with this dynamic, joyous, vital power which is in Jesus Christ. Nobody needs to be half-alive; everyone can live delightfully, with joyous vitality, if the relationship with Jesus is one of reality and is personal in nature.

To live with joyous vitality, practice is important. For if you practice being dead over a long period of time, you will be dead even while you live. If you practice being apathetic over a long period of time, you will become an apathetic personality. If you practice being unhappy, you will become unhappy.

Act as though you were filled with joy and vitality.

"Well," you might say, "that isn't honest, because I am not filled with joy."

But, yes, you are! It is below the surface of your nature waiting to be released. ". . . the kingdom of God is within you" (Luke 17:21). It is just that it has never come out. So act as though you had life and enthusiasm, as though you had health, as though you had talent, as though you had joy, and you will come to have them.

As William Barclay said:

> Prayer is not flight; prayer is power. Prayer does not deliver
> a man from some terrible situation; prayer enables a man to
> face and to master the situation.

And, of course, when one is able to master a difficult situation, he becomes joyful and life takes on brighter tones.

Proverbs are sayings that grow out of the long-accumulated wisdom of the human race. And therefore the old English proverb "Prayers should be the key of the day and the lock of the night" may be significant in that away back in time, spiritually minded people discovered that prayer gave enthusiasm for the day's work and peace filled with joy at eventide.

> Jesus has told us that when we learn to be perfect in
> thought, word and deed, that if we really try day after day,
> then we will discover God. Every good thought you have,

every good deed you do, every good secret desire of your heart is a whisper from God. Take time each hour of every day to contact God where you are, get an appointment with Him for one minute hourly, and day by day you will gain faith and conviction. Your thoughts, your whole personality, will change, for you will become, as Jesus, able to overcome all things in life.

Because God lives within you, then truth lives within you. His spirit is in you, His power is within you. Attend God every hour of your day, and the law of God will always work for you to bring you health, peace of mind and happiness.

The writer of the above, Dr. Albert E. Cliffe, often said that Jesus Christ is a scientist in that he teaches the workable formula of the good life, of joy, enthusiasm and peace of mind.

One of the happiest and most enthusiastic men I have ever known was Frank Bettger, whom I have quoted earlier. His joyful spirit and enthusiastic attitude derived from his profound faith, as indicated in the following story of a close call with death that he experienced. This was written many years ago in the early days of air travel:

Out on the Nevada desert one glorious moonlight night, just below the great Hoover Dam, on Lake Meade, I saw a strange phenomenon. I was stretched out on the flat of my back, looking up at a million stars. Guests of the Lake Meade Lodge had built a huge bonfire on the beach from driftwood . . . then I saw it! The smoke from that roaring fire was spiraling up into the sky from right to left, like the hands of a clock *turning backward!*

I had heard of this strange power caused by the rotation of the Earth; and I wondered why this same power causes smoke south of the Equator to *reverse* the action and spiral in the direction followed by the hands of a clock.

And it can never be different!

Likewise, the winds in a cyclone *north* of the Equator spiral counter clockwise; *south* of the Equator they spiral clockwise.

Lying there on the beach, gazing up at the stars and a beautiful full moon, I began wondering about the miracle of the Earth making a complete revolution—24,000 miles every 24 hours—right to the split second! "In addition to that," I got to thinking, "here we are, on the beach by this quiet lake, in perfect peace, yet this same power is carrying the Earth like a great space ship, on a complete round trip, circling the Sun every 365 days—the fantastic distance of *five hundred eighty-seven million miles every year!*"

. . . Not long afterward, I boarded a plane in Des Moines, Iowa, at seven o'clock in the morning. I was scheduled to speak that night in Toledo, Ohio. Shortly after we took off, a terrible wind and thunderstorm began tossing our two-motored plane around in the air. When we arrived over Chicago, a thick fog had blown in from the Great Lakes, bringing almost zero visibility. No incoming planes were permitted to land. After circling around more than an hour, the pilot announced that he had been instructed to go up to Milwaukee. When we reached Milwaukee, the fog was too heavy to make a landing there, so we were ordered to go on through to Toledo. But there, it was even worse, so we tried Cleveland. Same result. Great bolts of lightning flashed all around us. Violent thunderbolts shook the heavens. Our plane kept going, but no one seemed to know where.

Six o'clock that night, our pilot radioed the airport that our gas was running dangerously low. We were given the signal to descend. Everyone held his breath! Suddenly, we began bouncing on the ground, and the next thing we knew we came to a stop directly in front of the main building of the Cleveland Airport! Then, something happened in that plane I never saw happen before—nor since. Simultaneously, every one of us, twenty-four passengers, applauded! It was an applause quite different from any I ever heard before . . . I think we were all praying—not saying—"*Thank You God!*"—and "*Thank you!*" to the pilot.

I managed to get a sandwich and hot coffee at the lunch-counter. A westbound plane came in—the fog was lifting a bit, so they put me on. I arrived in Toledo just in time for the meeting. Three men were waiting at the airport to greet me. They had been there for hours.

As we drove out to the Scott High School Auditorium, where I was to make my talk, they told me the following extraordinary story:

"Gil" Dittmer, prominent insurance executive and chairman of this meeting, was giving a five-o'clock cocktail party at his home in my honor. Naturally, I was supposed to be there. Twelve committee members were enjoying a jolly party, because the meeting was a sell-out, and these men had all worked hard for it. But, as time went on, they began receiving frightening reports from the three members waiting at the airport. "One plane over Indiana crashed!" they said, "and Frank Bettger's plane is in trouble!" Later, when rumors started that the plane I was on was reported missing, the cocktail party developed into a *Prayer Meeting!*

"Some of those prayers," they told me later, "were the most fantastic God ever listened to, but we were all convinced that God heard us all right, because He never listened to more sincere, earnest praying!" One man declared, "A few of those prayers were delivered by men who hadn't prayed in years!"

I'm not recommending "cocktail party-prayer meetings" . . . but I must admit, I'll always feel highly honored by the one that was "rounded up" for me!

. . . Now, let me tell you about some of the thoughts I had up there in that plane. I had plenty of time to think. Eleven hours of it! During the worst part of the flight, I had a little prayer-meeting all of my own! I seemed to be listening for the most part. I heard nothing. Yet, a message seemed to come to me just as clearly as if I did hear it! It was in the form of questions . . . like this:

. . . "Remember that night in Nevada on the beach at Lake Meade, how you noticed the phenomenon of the smoke spiraling into the sky from right to left? . . . And how it dawned on you that the great Power controlling the movement of that smoke is the same Power which controls and navigates the Sun, the Stars, the Earth, and all the other planets? . . .

"That God created this power, and the Laws; and is directing all things on this earth. *He* has the only *Master Plan.* And *these* laws—man can never revoke . . . Remember?

"Do you know there is another great Law—created by this same Power—controlling the destiny of man—the *Law of Right and Wrong?*—and that this is another law man can never revoke? . . .

"Unknowingly—when you hit the sawdust trail and grasped Billy Sunday's hand, you were making a decision to harness your life to this *Great Power* . . . Since that day, some miraculous things have happened to the broken down ball-player that little mongrel brought away from the bridge in Chattanooga, Tennessee. . . ."

These were some of the thoughts that kept running through my head up there while we were being tossed around ten thousand feet in the air. Was I scared? Was I worried? Believe it or not—No! I had a strange feeling of security. I had a *job* to do. *This job.* And I believed I would be allowed to finish it. I believed this. I really did. I just *knew* I was going to get down out of that plane alive!

When I applauded *"Thank You!"* with all the other passengers, I wasn't applauding because fear had passed, and I was alive and breathing. I was saying *"Thank You!"* because I discovered my faith had been so real. I had experienced the Great Universal *Power of Faith!*

Another inspiring friend was Ralph Spaulding Cushman who wrote a poem that bubbled out of his faith-filled and joyous nature. It is called "The Secret." It is indeed a basic secret of living and one anyone can learn:

> I met God in the morning
>   When my day was at its best,
> And His presence came like sunrise,
>   Like a glory in my breast.
>
> All day long the Presence lingered,
>   All day long He stayed with me,
> And we sailed in perfect calmness
>   O'er a very troubled sea.

Other ships were blown and battered,
　　Other ships were sore distressed,
But the winds that seemed to drive them
　　Brought to us a peace and rest.

Then I thought of other mornings,
　　With a keen remorse of mind,
When I too had loosed the moorings,
　　With the Presence left behind.

So I think I know the secret,
　　Learned from many a troubled way:
You must seek Him in the morning
　　If you want Him through the day!

Dale Evans Rogers gives her own secret of the joy and enthusiasm which has filled her life despite some hard experiences. She says:

Prayer! I couldn't live without it; I would have died a dozen times if it had not been for my chance to talk it over with God, and gain strength in it from Him.

How can we know the mind and will of God? How can we know His plan for our daily lives? Deciding about that is most difficult, as all important decisions are difficult.

I think the best way to arrive at the right decision is to first pray about it, placing it in God's hands. Then sleep on it. The next morning, when you get up, I believe that the first solution that comes to your mind will be the right one—that is, if you have complete confidence in God's guidance. "But let him ask in faith, nothing wavering. For he that wavereth is like a wave of the sea driven with the wind and tossed" (*James* 1:6). Ask God's help in faith, and our decision will be right. I have found it unwise to make important decisions at the end of the day, when we are weary and tired. But once we have made a decision, we must not look back, like Lot's wife. We must act then on the faith that God has given us the answer—and know that only good will come out of it.

Since prayer is a basic way to deal with life's problems and a source of wisdom and peace and joy, I have practiced nine prayer steps suggested by my friend, Dr. Charles L. Allen. These nine steps will work when practiced:

To make the most of prayer, let me suggest nine prayer steps.

There are three steps to take *before* prayer:

(1) Decide what you really want. Get clearly in mind exactly what you plan to ask in prayer.

(2) Seek to determine whether or not what you want is right. Ask yourself such questions as: Is it fair to everyone else concerned? Is it best for me? Is it in harmony with the Spirit of God?

(3) Write it down. Reducing our requests to writing helps to clarify our thinking and deepen the impressions upon our mind and heart.

Then, there are three steps to take *during* prayer:

(1) Keep the mind still. Just as the moon cannot be perfectly reflected on a restless sea, so God cannot be experienced by an unquiet mind. "Be still, and know that I am God" (Psalm 46:10). At this point we must concentrate to keep the mind from wandering.

(2) Talk *with* God, and not *to* God. Instead of saying, with Samuel, "Speak; for thy servant heareth" (1 Samuel 3:10), we are prone to say, "Listen, Lord, for Thy servant speaketh." Prayer is both speaking and listening.

(3) Promise God what you yourself will do to answer your own prayer. God answers prayer, not for you, but with you. Jesus performed many of His miracles by giving the person to be helped something to do. As you pray, search for the things that you yourself can do.

Then, there are three steps to take *after* prayer:

(1) Always remember to thank God for answering your prayer. You would not pray in the first place if you did not believe God would answer. Now, confirm that belief by thanking Him for the answer, even though it has not yet come.

(2) Be willing to accept whatever God's answer may be, remembering the words of our Lord, ". . . nevertheless not my will, but thine, be done" (Luke 22:42).

(3) Do everything loving that comes to your mind. One of the objects of prayer is to bring the love of God into our hearts; and as we express that love, we make it possible for God to answer our prayers better.

And it is to our advantage to remember, especially whenever the going gets hard, some reassuring words from Psalms 145:18:

> The Lord is nigh unto all them that call upon him, to all that call upon him in truth.

That reassurance will keep your faith going even when doubts tend to creep in as to whether God is there listening to you. As Helen Steiner Rice so touchingly puts it:

> GOD, ARE YOU THERE?
> I'm way down HERE!
> You're way up THERE!
> Are You sure You can hear
> My faint, faltering prayer?
> For I'm so unsure
> Of just how to pray—
> To tell you the truth, God,
> I don't know what to say . . .
> I just know I am lonely
> And vaguely disturbed,
> Bewildered and restless,
> Confused and perturbed . . .
> And they tell me that prayer
> Helps to quiet the mind
> And to unburden the heart
> For in stillness we find
> A newborn assurance
> That SOMEONE DOES CARE
> And SOMEONE DOES ANSWER
> Each small sincere prayer!

Apparently human beings have always turned their thoughts and prayers to the Great Divinity which they perceived in the structure of the world, in its beauty, and in the power and majesty of nature. And from that source they drew strength and the power to live greatly. Something of these thoughts is in this prayer of a Chippewa Indian:

> O Great Spirit, whose voice I hear in the woods and whose breath gives life to all the world, hear me. I am a man before you, one of your many children. I am small and weak. I need your strength and wisdom. Let me walk in beauty, and make my eyes ever behold the red and purple sunsets. Make my hands respect the things you have made, my ears sharp to hear your voice. Make me wise so that I may know the things you have taught my people, the lessons you have hid in every leaf and rock. I seek strength, O Great Spirit of my fathers— not to be superior to my brothers, but to be able to fight my greatest enemy, myself.
>
> Make me ever ready to come to you with clean hands and a straight eye, so that when life fades like a fading sunset, my spirit may come to you without shame.

The elevated insights contained in the prayer of the Indian are also present in a medieval prayer, the author's name unknown as far as I am able to ascertain:

> Almighty God, Father, Son, and Spirit, who art power, wisdom, and love, inspire in us those same three things:
>
> power to serve Thee,
> wisdom to please Thee,
> and love to accomplish Thy will;
> power that I may do,
> wisdom that I may know what to do,
> and love that I may be moved to do all
>   that is pleasing to Thee.

Always we find as we read in the literature of prayer and devotion that spiritual upthrust comes through, and invariably those who practice in-depth quality prayer are joyful, peaceful, enthusiastic and even radiant people. It all seems to indicate that a close relationship exists between the love and daily living with God and the quality of happiness. Rufus M. Jones, one of the outstanding spiritual leaders of our time, even goes so far as to say that communion with God is the solution of all our troubles. He states:

LIVING COMMUNION

The solution of all our troubles and problems is, I maintain, to be found in the recovery of more vital methods of living communion with God. It would be well for us to reduce the amount of talk, of words, of argument, of question-asking, reduce also what is formal and mechanical, and greatly increasing the living, silent, penetrating corporate activity of worship of which Whittier wrote those great words of his— the meaning of which he had experienced:

> "Without spoken words, low breathings stole
> Of a diviner life from soul to soul,
> Baptizing in one tender thought the whole."

And Louis Cassels writes on the same theme:

That doughty Christian, St. Theresa of Avila, speaks of "the dark night of the soul." She was referring to an experience shared by all who travel more than a few steps along the Christian way. The traditional name for the experience is "doubt." But in this context the word has a special meaning.

It does not necessarily imply that you are plunged into intellectual doubt about the existence of God. It means, rather, that you suddenly feel bereft of a sense of his presence which hitherto has been very real to you. The feeling is one of acute loss, almost of bereavement.

What brings on "the dark night of the soul"? It may be simply an expression of great fatigue—mental, emotional, or physical. It may be the result of allowing the mind to wander too far from the things that really matter and becoming too preoccupied with the cares and pleasures of everyday life. But in some cases, it seems to be God himself who deliberately withdraws the consciousness of his presence from these who are accustomed to being sustained by it.

Why does God do this? George Macdonald offered this guess: "He wants to make us in his own image, choosing the good, refusing the evil. How should He effect this if He were *always* moving us from within, as He does at divine intervals, towards the beauty of holiness?" In other words, God withdraws in order to give us the freedom of choosing anew whether we will pursue him above all else.

What can a person do when he finds his prayers bouncing back from the ceiling? Macdonald has this advice: "Fold the arms of your faith and wait in quietness until the light goes up in your darkness. Fold the arms of your faith, I say, but not of your action. Think of something you ought to do, and go do it. Heed not your feelings. Do your work."

Perhaps a reason that prayer and faith produce an upthrust of joy is the fact of their powerful working in sickness and suffering.

A passage in the Book of James (5:13–16) deals with this matter:

Is any among you afflicted? let him pray. Is any merry? let him sing psalms.

Is any sick among you? let him call for the elders of the church; and let them pray over him, anointing him with oil in the name of the Lord:

And the prayer of faith shall save the sick, and the Lord shall raise him up; and if he have committed sins, they shall be forgiven him.

Confess your faults one to another, and pray one for another, that ye may be healed. The effectual fervent prayer of a righteous man availeth much.

I have the habit of keeping stories I have read and often they have come to good use in helping others. Here is one that concerns three young fellows who discovered the upthrust of spirit that comes from prayer and the Bible. Actually their lives were saved by it. It was written by Robert Trumbull:

(Early in 1942, Americans read with pride and admiration the short news-paper accounts of three Navy fliers who fought the sea for thirty-four days, while they drifted in a rubber raft without food, equipment, and for some time without clothes, yet survived to land, weak and bent, on a strange shore.)

Before evening, the three of us were sitting dejectedly si-lent. Then Gene made a suggestion.

"It might be a good idea," he said, not meeting our eyes, "to say a prayer."

We discussed this seriously. We found that we had all been reared in some religious atmosphere, but that we had all drifted away. It had been many years since I had been inside a civilian church, but I sometimes attended Sunday services held by the chaplain aboard ship, when my duties permitted and I was not going ashore.

We all concluded that a word of prayer wouldn't hurt any-thing.

So we sat in the steaming little cup that our boat had be-come, and bowed our heads beneath the cruel tropic sun. We each mumbled a few words of our own awkward choosing, calling on our God to bless our loved ones back home, over whom we were more concerned than ourselves, and asking for a little rain.

We were all quite skeptical about the possibility of any an-swer to our prayer.

"Well, now we done all we could," Tony said.

"Gee, give it a chance," Gene answered impatiently. I called on my store of proverbs.

"God helps those that help themselves," I said.

"Well, come on, rain," Tony challenged. "Or maybe it ain't gonna rain no mo', no mo'."

We lifted our voices lustily at that and sang, "It Ain't Gonna Rain No Mo'," as far as we knew the words—which wasn't far—as if by our false cynicism we could put a reverse hoodoo on the elements.

At least we were all laughing again, which we hadn't done for some time.

Despite our elaborate irreverence, there was no denying

that the prayer had made us feel better. Gene, who had more piety in his nature than either Tony or I, took evident satisfaction. His mind now was obviously clean of worries or self-reproaches.

That night it rained.

We had another prayer meeting that night, and every night thereafter. Each evening, after the sun's flamboyant departure left us feeling more alone in a world that suddenly lost all color, we devoted perhaps an hour to our informal service. There was a comfort in passing our burden to Someone bigger than we in this empty vastness. Further, the common devotion drew us together, since it seemed that we no longer depended entirely upon each other, but could appeal, simultaneously, to a Fourth that we three held equally in reverence.

After our halting prayers—neither Gene nor I was scholarly in formal religion, and Tony could pray only in Polish—we developed naturally the "fellowship period" familiar to those who have attended Protestant Sunday school.

We sang some popular songs, a time or two. I couldn't remember any except old ones. I hadn't been to a dance, except occasionally, in twelve or fifteen years, and popular songs go away from me. The songs that I knew, the boys had never heard. The more recent ones that they could sing, I couldn't. However, we managed to get together on a few, and that gave us a lift.

It was later that I came to realize how little we knew about the Bible. One night, after our prayer meeting, I told a Bible story. Appropriately, it was the miracle of the loaves and fishes.

The boys were tickled with it. In my youth I had been brought up in a denomination of the church that holds regular Sunday school, so I drew upon a long memory. Of course, the stories were in my own improvised words. I hadn't been to church for many years, so it's easy to imagine how good I was at recalling the stories I had learned as a youngster. I hadn't been inside a civilian church since 1923, when I was back home after my first cruise. Aboard ship, the chapel services which I occasionally attended included everything but Bible stories.

My religious training had been such that I could now recall all the favorite stories of the Scriptures, but nowhere near verbatim. Gene recalled a number of stories, but couldn't tell them. He would think of a story, and then it would be up to me to tell it.

Tony had never heard any of these things before. In his church, all the services were in Polish—or Latin. The best-known Biblical tales were all new to him. He begged me every night to tell him more and more.

Well, I didn't want to tell him everything I knew in one night, so each evening I'd tell one story. That went on until the end.

I found my recollections of the Bible very useful in the last week or ten days, when we were all exhibiting a tendency to brood over our position. One of my hazy parables would snap us out of our depression and start a flood of discussion in which our dismal outlook was momentarily forgotten.

Many a time I wished a preacher, or someone well versed in Scripture, were present. The wording I used would certainly shock a Bible student.

We finally landed on an island through a jagged and dangerous reef. The commissioner was curious as to how we had reached this particular part of the island. Had we walked there? We merely turned and pointed seaward. He was astounded. That, he said, was impossible! He could not believe we had come upon this beach from the sea. No one had ever come over that reef and lived to tell the tale!

It was our turn to be astonished. But after a surprised glance at each other, we pointed to our little raft, tied to the piling near the shack.

In all, we covered approximately one thousand miles in the raft, but actually, from the point at which we landed our plane to this island the distance was about 750 miles.

Joy is basic in the teachings of Jesus. "These things," He said, "have I spoken unto you . . . that your joy might be full (John 15:11). He knew that joy "doeth good like a medicine" (Proverbs 17:22) and He was a teacher of those attitudes and thoughts that lead to joy and enthusiasm.

So the advice of Hermas, early Christian writer and wise man that he was, deserves to be heeded:

> Put sadness away from thee, for truly sadness is the sister of half-heartedness and bitterness. Array thee in the joy that always finds favour in God's sight and is acceptable with him; yea, revel thou therein. For everyone that is joyous worketh and thinketh those things that are good, and despiseth sadness. But he that is sad doth always wickedly; first because he maketh sad the Holy Spirit that hath been given to man for joy; and secondly he worketh lawlessness, in that he neither prays to God nor gives him thanks. Therefore cleanse thyself from this wicked sadness, and thou shalt live with God. Yea, unto God all they shall live who have cast out sadness from themselves, and arrayed themselves in all joy.

8

Keep Your Spirit Built Up

FRANK BETTGER WRITES:

> Make a high and holy resolve that you will double the amount of enthusiasm that you have been putting into your work and into your life! . . . If you carry out that resolve . . . be prepared to see astonishing results. It will probably double your income, and double your happiness.
>
> "If you can give your son or daughter only one gift,
> let it be Enthusiasm!"   —BRUCE BARTON

That is wise advice. In his day Bruce Barton, one of the nation's leading advertising executives, influenced the attitudes and therefore the lives of thousands of people through his books, articles and speeches. He knew the importance of enthusiasm as a sort of mental and spiritual fire which burns off the negative attitudes and makes it possible for positive concepts to become dominant and therefore determinative. He believed in the constant build-up and refreshing of the spirit.

And I am sure that the man who has been called the wisest American would agree with the foregoing high appraisal of the value of enthusiasm, for Ralph Waldo Emerson said:

Nothing great was ever achieved without enthusiasm.

But enthusiasm can run down lest you keep joy going strong. For enthusiasm thrives on joy. But there are always hardships, frustrations and failures ready to attack our joy and undercut enthusiasm.

Ella Wheeler Wilcox, whose poetry has delighted and inspired millions, had something to say on this problem:

> Fate used me meanly; but I looked at her and laughed,
> That none might know how bitter was the cup I quaffed.
> Along came Joy, and paused beside me where I sat,
> Saying, "I came to see what you were laughing at."

Albert E. Cliffe agrees with Ella Wheeler Wilcox when he says:

> You know you sometimes think yourself into unhappiness, into a depression. Do you know that you can also think yourself into gladness? It is by such thinking that you get well, that you prosper, that your prayers are always answered. Become the master of your own thinking. Stop thinking about how tough life is to you, stop thinking about the future and the past, think of God's riches and love, try to express such thoughts from day to day. You will become whatever you think.

And I like the statement relative to the build-up of joy and enthusiasm made by Emily M. Bishop in her book called *The Road to Seventy Years Young:*

> The best mental tonic for the vital processes are the habits of cheer and courage. Not "spells" of happy confidence which are more than offset by "spells" of doubt, of timidity and of poisonous fear, but *an habitually positive cheer-courage outlook*. Of course, thinking and feeling are not strictly voluntary acts, but it lies within the domain of one's volitional power to select the kind of thoughts and feelings which shall receive hospitable encouragement.

Many years ago in Cornwall there was a preacher who associated with John Wesley named Billy Bray. He was a man of powerful spiritual gifts who came out of a hard life in the tinworks of that area of England. In his own inimitable way, when he heard someone telling a long story about troubles and sorrows, his remark was: "I've had my trials and troubles. The Lord has given me both vinegar and honey, but He has given me the vinegar with a teaspoon and the honey with a ladle."

Margaret E. Sangster echoed the spirit of the Cornish miner-preacher in joyous words. She found this to be a great and wonderful world, which is a true insight that certainly vies with the so-called profundity that sees everything as bad—very bad:

> This beautiful world! This joyous life! I wonder if we are as happy and light of heart as we ought to be, we children dwelling even here in our Father's house. Most of us need, after youth is past, to cultivate a mood not only of contentment but of gaiety, and to make it the dominant note of our days. . . .
>
> Notice, the joys far outnumber the sorrows. Though the latter come in groups on occasion, they are exceptional, and whether occurring singly or together, they are offset by a long procession of calm and halcyon days, weeks, months and years, years which the Psalmist had in mind when he said, "I will remember the years of the right hand of the Most High."

Once my wife, Ruth, and I went out with a native driver onto the Serengeti plains in Africa for a period of two weeks. For that length of time we were entirely separated from newspapers, radio and television. At first we missed the news acutely, for are we not victims of the fast-paced, breathless media? But after a few days our attitude was one of "So what?" and finally even "Couldn't care less." And when, after fourteen days, we returned to a city and grabbed for a newspaper, we found that despite its big headlines and aside from a few details, the news wasn't all that different from two weeks before.

Our fortnight with the impalas, elephants, giraffes, wildebeests and lions of the Serengeti had done something deep and quiet and perhaps philosophical to us. Association with God's creatures had certainly given our inner joy and enthusiasm a definite build-up. Actually, we were not as sure as we had been just who had the best civilization—the men or the animals.

Indeed, the so-called lesser creatures may, through intuition or instinct, often come upon truth in deeper insight. Mark Guy Pearse says it in his poem "Don't Trouble Trouble":

Don't you trouble trouble till trouble troubles you.
Don't you look for trouble; let trouble look for you.
Who feareth hath forsaken the heavenly Father's side;
What He hath undertaken He surely will provide.

The very birds reprove thee with their happy song;
The very flowers teach thee that fretting is a wrong.
"Cheer up," the sparrow chirpeth; "Thy Father feedeth me;
Think how much He careth, oh, lonely child, for thee."

"Fear not," the flowers whisper; "since thus He hath arrayed
The buttercup and daisy, how canst thou be afraid?"
Then don't you trouble trouble till trouble troubles you;
You'll only double trouble, and trouble others too.

And in this connection I like "The Creed for Optimists" stated by Christian D. Larsen:

1. Promise yourself to be so strong that nothing can disturb your peace of mind.

2. Promise yourself to talk health, happiness and prosperity to every person you meet.

3. Promise yourself to make all your friends feel that there is something in them.

4. Promise yourself to look at the sunny side of everything and make your optimism come true.

5. Promise yourself to think only of the best, to work only for the best, and to expect only the best.

6. Promise yourself to be just as enthusiastic about the success of others as you are about your own.

7. Promise yourself to forget the mistakes of the past and to press on to the greater achievements of the future.

8. Promise yourself to wear a friendly countenance at all times and give every living creature you meet a smile.

9. Promise yourself to spend so much time improving yourself that you have no time left to criticize others.

10. Promise yourself to be too large for worry, too noble for anger, too strong for fear, and too happy to permit the presence of trouble.

A sure way to go about building up your joy and enthusiasm is to bypass your own troubles and get under the burdens of other people. It is surprising how the doing of that makes one glad. As Arnold Bennett so well said:

The best cure for worry, depression, melancholy, brooding, is to go deliberately forth and try to lift with one's sympathy the gloom of somebody else.

Helen Steiner Rice writes:

The more you love, the more you'll find
That life is good and friends are kind
For only what we give away
Enriches us from day to day.

So when we give away ourselves to get free of ourselves in being helpful to the less fortunate, we receive in return at least two magnificent gifts: a deep inner joy and a brand new enthusiasm for life and for people.

And I believe there is a subtle joy secret, a spiritual upthrust of happiness, in Grace Noll Crowell's lines:

I SHALL BE GLAD

If I can put new hope within the heart
Of one who has lost hope,
If I can help a brother up
Some difficult long slope
That seems too steep for tired feet to go,
If I can help him climb
Into the light upon the hill's far crest,
I shall begrudge no time

Or strength that I can spend, for well I know
How great may be his need.
If I can help through any darkened hour,
I shall be glad indeed.

For I recall how often I have been
Distressed, distraught, dismayed,
And hands have reached to help, and voices called
That kept me unafraid.
If I can share this help that I have had,
God knows I shall be glad.

It is a fact, of course, that love is a basic source of happiness and the zest for life. Whenever one is captured, that person is bound to find a whole new and exciting world and becomes capable of a new sensitivity to people, to beauty, to everything enthralling everywhere. I wonder if you remember that book of years ago *Good-Bye Mr. Chips* by James Hilton. It was read through laughter and some tears by multitudes. Mr. Chipping (Chips), the delightful master at Brookfield, an old English school, came to be loved by everyone, and it was because love made him joyful, and he in turn transmitted joy to all who came under the charm of his personality. Here are a few excerpts from this heartwarming story:

> . . . his marriage was a triumphant success. Katherine conquered Brookfield as she had conquered Chips; she was immensely popular with boys and masters alike. Even the wives of the masters, tempted at first to be jealous of one so young and lovely, could not long resist her charms. . . .
>
> But most remarkable of all was the change she made in Chips. Till his marriage he had been a dry and rather neutral sort of person; liked and thought well of by Brookfield in general, but not of the stuff that makes for great popularity or that stirs great affection . . . now came love, the sudden love of boys for a man who was kind without being soft, who understood them well enough, but not too much, and whose private happiness linked them with their own. He began to make little jokes, the sort that schoolboys like—mnemonics and puns

that raised laughs and at the same time imprinted something in the mind. . . .

[Mr. Chips is called out of retirement during World War I and when the Head of Brookfield dies, he is made Acting Head of Brookfield, "for the duration."]

He was a grand success altogether. In some strange way he did, and they all knew and felt it, help things. For the first time in his life he felt *necessary*—and necessary to something that was nearest his heart. There is no sublimer feeling in the world, and it was his at last.

He made new jokes, too—about the O.T.C. and the food-rationing system and the anti-air-raid blinds that had to be fitted on all the windows. There was a mysterious kind of rissole that began to appear on the School menu on Mondays, and Chips called it abhorrendum—"meat to be abhorred." The story went round—heard Chips's latest? . . .

Laughter . . . laughter . . . wherever he went and whatever he said, there was laughter. He had earned the reputation of being a great jester, and jests were expected of him. Whenever he rose to speak at a meeting, or even when he talked across a table, people prepared their minds and faces for the joke. They listened in a mood to be amused and it was easy to satisfy them. They laughed sometimes before he came to the point. "Old Chips was in fine form," they would say, afterward. "Marvelous the way he can always see the funny side of things. . . ."

[After another retirement he still keeps in touch with the current students as well as former ones. They drop in for tea and he is over at Brookfield frequently.]

About a quarter to four a ring came, and Chips, answering the front door himself (which he oughtn't to have done), encountered a rather small boy wearing a Brookfield cap and an expression of anxious timidity. "Please, sir," he began, "does Mr. Chips live here?"

"Umph—you'd better come inside," Chips answered. And in his room a moment later he added: "I am—umph—the person you want. Now what can I—umph—do for you?"

"I was told you wanted me, sir."

Chips smiled. An old joke—an old leg-pull, and he, of all
people, having made so many old jokes in his time, ought not
to complain. And it amused him to cap their joke, as it were,
with one of his own; to let them see that he could keep his
end up, even yet. So he said, with eyes twinkling: "Quite
right, my boy. I wanted you to take tea with me. Will you—
umph—sit down by the fire? Umph—I don't think I have seen
your face before. How is that?"

"I've only just come out of the sanatorium, sir—I've been
there since the beginning of term with measles."

"Ah, that accounts for it."

Chips began his usual ritualistic blending of tea from the
different caddies; luckily there was half a walnut cake with
pink icing in the cupboard. He found out that the boy's name
was Linford, that he lived in Shropshire, and that he was the
first of his family at Brookfield.

"You know—umph—Linford—you'll like Brookfield—
when you get used to it. It's not half such an awful place—as
you imagine. You're a bit afraid of it—um, yes—eh? So was
I, my dear boy—at first. But that was—um—a long time ago.
Sixty-three years ago—umph—to be precise. When I—um—
first went into Big Hall and—um—I saw all those boys—I tell
you—I was quite scared. Indeed—umph—I don't think I've
ever been so scared in my life. Not even when—umph—the
Germans bombed us—during the War. But—umph—it didn't
last long—the scared feeling, I mean. I soon made myself—
um—at home."

"Were there a lot of other new boys that term, sir?" asked
Linford shyly.

"Eh? But—God bless my soul—I wasn't a boy at all—I was
a man—a young man of twenty-two! And the next time you
see a young man—a new master—taking his first prep in Big
Hall—umph—just think—what it feels like!"

"But if you were twenty-two then, sir—"

"Yes? Eh?"

"You must be—very old—now, sir."

Chips laughed quietly and steadily to himself. It was a good joke.

"Well—umph—I'm certainly—umph—no chicken."

There is still another source one can call upon to help keep the spirit built up and that is good old nature, the great mother and teacher of us all. There one can, if one will listen, and look, and meditate, find the great and loving God, the Creator of nature, who speaks to every seeking heart through His marvelous, powerful and exquisite handiwork.

Anne Frank found it so despite the tragedies:

> The best remedy for those who are afraid, lonely or unhappy is to go outside, somewhere where they can be quite alone with the heavens, nature, and God. Because only then does one feel that all is as it should be and that God wishes to see people happy, amidst the simple beauty of nature. As long as this exists, and it certainly always will, I know that then there will always be comfort for every sorrow, whatever the circumstances may be.

I believe it was Emerson who said, "The sky is the daily bread of the eyes." I recall one crystal-clear, crisp day on the far western prairie when I became acutely conscious of the vast, unobstructed expanse of the sky from horizon to horizon. I watched it for hours—the changing light and shadow, the appearance and disappearance of fleecy clouds now enormous, now small floating ships of white in a great canopy of blue. It was indeed food for the eyes and the soul.

Alfred Kreymborg has a line that is memorable and it makes one glad just to read it:

> The sky is that beautiful old parchment in which the sun and the moon keep their diary.

And John Ruskin, whose garden I have several times visited in northern England, reminds us that:

> Nature is painting for us, day after day, pictures of infinite beauty if only we have eyes to see them.

That thought about the sky being food for the soul is echoed by Luther Burbank, who said:

> Flowers always make people better, happier and more helpful; they are sunshine, food and medicine to the soul.

As a student in college I fell under the charm of the English poet William Wordsworth and have several times journeyed to Tintern Abbey, that storied and romantic ruin on the river Wye in Wales. C. S. Lewis describes it well:

> It is an abbey practically intact except that the roof is gone, and the glass out of the windows, and the floor instead of a pavement is a trim green lawn. Anything like the sweetness and peace of the long shafts of sunlight falling through the windows on the grass cannot be imagined. All churches should be roofless. A holier place I never saw.

Always at Tintern Abbey I have shared Wordsworth's feeling of joy and deeply moving inspiration which he describes in a famous sentence:

> . . . And I have felt
> A presence that disturbs me with the
>   joy
> Of elevated thoughts; . . .

Again and still again I have visited the poet's cottage at Grassmere and have wandered over the Lake district at daffodil time looking for the spot where he saw "a crowd, a host, of golden daffodils." And I will always believe I found the spot on that sun-swept day when, by Ullswater, I saw *my* crowd of daffodils "beside the lake, beneath the trees, fluttering and dancing in the breeze."

Man is nature's child and therefore God's child. And when he turns for a build-up of spirit to the woods and seas and waterfalls and meadows lying in the sun, the upthrust will come surging into his heart.

Faith is the great restorer of spirit. When one has faith nothing can crush him—not even death itself. For faith gives the glorious insight that life in spirit is deathless. ". . . because I live, ye shall live also" (John 14:19).

For years I have been recording a series of incidents which bear out the conviction that life, not death, is the basic principle of our universe. From them I have gained the unshakable belief that there is no death, that here and hereafter are one. When I reached this conclusion, I found it to be the most satisfying and convincing philosophy of my entire life. Following are the experiences which convinced me that human spirits on both sides of death live in a fellowship that continues unbroken.

H. B. Clarke, an old friend of mine, was of a scientific turn of mind, restrained, factual, unemotional. I was called one night by his physician, who expected him to live only a few hours.

I prayed for him, as did others. The next day his eyes opened and after a few days he recovered his speech. His heart action returned to normal. After he recovered strength he said, "At some time during my illness something very peculiar happened to me. It seemed that I was a long distance away, in the most beautiful and attractive place I have ever seen. There were lights all about me. I saw faces dimly revealed—kind faces they were—and I felt peaceful and happy. In fact, I never felt happier.

"The thought came, 'I must be dying.' Then it occurred to me, 'Perhaps I have died.' I almost laughed out loud, and asked myself, 'Why have I been afraid of death all my life? There is nothing to be afraid of in this.' "

"Did you want to live?" I asked.

He smiled and said, "It did not make the slightest difference. If anything, I think I would have preferred to stay in that beautiful place."

Hallucination? A dream? A vision? I do not believe so. I have spent too many years talking to people who have come to the edge of "something" and had a look across, who unanimously have reported beauty, light and peace, to have any doubt in my mind.

A member of my church, Mrs. Bryson Kalt, tells of an aunt whose husband and three children were burned to death when their house was destroyed by fire. The aunt was badly burned but lived for three years. When finally she lay dying, a radiance suddenly came over her face. "It is all so beautiful," she said. "They are coming to meet me. Fluff up my pillows and let me go to sleep."

Friends of mine, Mr. and Mrs. William Sage, lived in New Jersey and I was often in their home. Then Will Sage died. A few years later, when Mrs. Sage was on her deathbed, the most surprised look passed across her face. It lighted up in a wonderful smile as she said, "Why, it is Will!" That she saw him those about her bed had no doubt whatsoever.

The late Rufus Jones had a son, Lowell, the apple of his eye. The boy became sick when Dr. Jones was on the ocean, bound for Europe. The night before entering Liverpool, while lying in his bunk, Dr. Jones experienced an indefinable, unexplainable sadness. Then, he said, he seemed to be enveloped in the arms of God. A great feeling of peace and a sense of profound possession of his son came to him.

Upon landing in Liverpool, he was advised that Lowell had died; the death had occurred at the exact moment when Dr. Jones had felt God's presence and the everlasting nearness of his son.

A boy serving in the war in Korea wrote to his mother, saying, "The strangest things happen to me. Once in a while at night, when I am afraid, Dad seems to be with me." His father had been dead for ten years. "Do you think that Dad can actually be with me here on these Korean battlefields?"

Why not? How can we not believe that this could be true? Again and again proofs are offered that this universe is a great spiritual sounding house, alive and vital.

My mother was a great soul, and her influence on me will ever stand out in my life as an experience that cannot be surpassed. During my adult years, whenever I had the opportunity, I went home to see her. It was always an exciting experience.

Then came her death, and in the fullness of summertime we tenderly laid her body in the beautiful little cemetery at Lynchburg in southern Ohio, a town where she had lived as a girl.

It came autumn, and I felt that I wanted to be with my mother again. I was lonely without her, so I went to Lynchburg. The weather was cold and the sky overcast as I walked to the cemetery. I pushed through the old iron gates and my feet rustled in the leaves as I walked to her grave, where I sat sad and lonely. But of a sudden the clouds parted and the sun came through.

Then I seemed to hear her voice. The message was clear and distinct, stated in her beloved old-time tone: "Why seek ye the living among the dead? I am not here. I am with you and my loved ones always."

In a burst of inner light I became wondrously happy. I knew that what I had heard was the truth. I stood up and put my hand on the tombstone and saw it for what it was: only a place where mortal remains lay. But she, that gloriously lovely spirit, is still with us, her loved ones.

The New Testament teaches the indestructibility of life. It describes Jesus after His Crucifixion in a series of disappearances and reappearances. This indicates He is trying to tell us that when we do not see Him, it does not mean He is not there. Out of sight does not mean out of life.

The mystical appearances which some of us today experience indicate the same truth: that He is near. Did He not say, "Because I live, ye shall live also"? In other words, our loved ones who have died in this faith are also nearby, and occasionally draw near to comfort us.

The Bible gives other insights into the great question, "What happens when a man leaves this world?" And it wisely tells us that we know these truths by faith. The surest way into truth, says Henri Bergson, the philosopher, is by perception, by intuition; by reasoning to a certain point, then taking a "mortal leap." You come to that glorious moment when you simply "know" the truth.

Of these deep and tender matters I have no doubt whatsoever. I firmly believe in the continuation of life after what we call death takes place. I believe there are two sides to the phenomenon known as death: this side where we now live, and the other side where we shall continue to live. Eternity does not start with death. We are in eternity now. We merely change the form of the experience called life—and that change, I am persuaded, is for the better.

Recently I read a curious but fascinating dissertation called "Wise Animals I Have Known" by Alan Devoe. Animals, as I have observed them, are not tense or worried. They seem quietly and calmly to live under the protection of God. And it is wonderful how animals seem to avoid being infected by the uptightness of humans. Living with them makes its contribution to the uplifted spirit:

If I live to be 80 and still greet the morning with a praise like prayer, it will not be from anything I have read in books of philosophy. It will be because I knew animals.

They are very close, said Saint Francis, to the paternal heart of God. I think they must be. By instinct an animal puts infinite trust in life.

This morning at sunrise I watched Thomas, our cat, greet the new day. Thomas is now (in human terms) going on for 80. Every morning I share daybreak with him. It is great medicine. First there is his rush up the cellar stairs, lithe and springy as a tiger, from the place where he sleeps by the furnace. While I fix his food I watch him. He always begins with the ritual of str-*etch*-ing. Nothing trivial or hasty, mind you, but a leisurely, carefully relished luxury that does him as much good as a vacation. Left front paw, right front paw, now both hind legs, now a long bend of the back . . . *aaah!* A brisk shake; the big green eyes open wide; the ears perk up.

He dashes to the French window, rears up with forepaws on the glass, and peers out all quivering and tail twitching with excitement. Sunshine! Trees! Great heaven, there is a leaf blowing hop-skip across the lawn! Thomas has looked out through this same pane hundreds of mornings, but every time it is fresh and challenging and wonderful.

And so with breakfast. You'd think he had never seen this old chipped dish before. He pounces on his food like a man finding uranium. Then, when the last bit has been neatly licked from the plate, comes the ecstatic moment for going out to the new day.

Thomas never just goes through the doorway. (Animals don't take these moments lightly.) First he glides *half*way through, then stands drinking in the sounds, scents, sights out there. Another inch or two and he stands again. At last, very slowly, he slips over the threshold. If so much wonder were to hit Thomas all at once he could hardly stand it.

Now he rushes to the middle of the lawn and there this octogenarian performs a riotous caper. He takes a flying jump at nothing in particular, then zigzags after nonexistent mice. He leaps in the air and claps his paws on invisible butterflies. Then some quick flip-flops, rolling over and over, all four paws waving. In a minute it is finished and he steps gravely off to his day's adventures.

What better lesson in living could one have? Here is joy in every moment, an awareness of the electric excitement of the earth and all that's in it. One further lesson from Thomas: when he sleeps, he *sleeps*. He curls up in a ball, puts one paw over the top of his head and turns himself over to God.

All animals give themselves wholeheartedly to the joy of being. At dusk in my woods flying squirrels play aerial roller-coaster. I have seen an old fox batting a stick in absorbed rapture for half an hour. Children react thus simply to the world about them, before reason steps in to complicate their lives. . . .

If animals can be said to have a philosophy, it is as simple as this: When Nature says, "I give you the glory of the senses and of awareness, and the splendor of earth," surrender yourself to these things, not worrying if it looks undignified to turn somersaults at 80. When the word is "Fight!" pitch in and fight, not weighing hesitant thoughts about prudence.

"Rest," says your monitor. "Play." "Sleep." "Feed and breed and doze in God's green shade by the brookside," each in its season. Heed the voice and act. It is a simple philosophy. It holds the strength of the world.

Animals do not know worry. . . .

An animal doesn't know what brotherhood means, but when it hears the call "Help!" it answers instinctively. . . .

Not only do the wild things meet life in all its aspects wholeheartedly; they greet death the same way. "Sleep now, and rest," says Nature at the end. . . .

In animals shines the trust that casts out fear.

I have always observed that people who keep company with the natural world, who live with mountains, plains, lakes, with the sun and the wind, the moon and the stars, are peaceful, joyous men and women, and they are nourished in their souls by a spirit that can flow only from God. So John Muir writes:

> Climb the mountains and get their good tidings. Nature's peace will flow into you as sunshine flows into trees. The winds will flow their own freshness into you and the storms their energy, while cares will drop off like autumn leaves.

The greatest of all earthly mysteries perhaps lies in the astonishing potential built into a person that can be released by a change to a positive attitude. As William James said:

> The greatest discovery of my generation is that human beings can alter their lives by altering their attitudes of mind.

Finally, to help in always keeping a built-up spirit, I give you three of the great promises that lead to a joyous and enthusiastic life:

> . . . In the world ye shall have tribulation: but be of good cheer; I have overcome the world.
>
> John 16:33

> Hitherto have ye asked nothing in my name: ask, and ye shall receive, that your joy may be full.
>
> John 16:24

> Jesus said unto him, If thou canst believe, all things are possible to him that believeth.
>
> Mark 9:23

9

Joy and Enthusiasm in a World of Beauty

"THIS IS THE DAY which the Lord hath made; we will rejoice and be glad in it." So says Psalms 118:24.

I have recommended that one magnificent salutation to the day to thousands of people in scores of audiences across the land and in foreign nations for many years. And I can factually and gratefully report that it has changed lives wherever it has become part of the daily experience. It has helped make happy and positive individuals out of those who previously had been desultory, defeated and negative. These people have discovered that the practice of a joyous and enthusiastic attitude every day results in one's days becoming so conditioned.

For one thing, such a positive attitude puts one into harmony with this world of beauty, with nature itself. The famous London preacher who creatively touched the lives of thousands a century ago expressed this harmony in an impressive statement. Charles H. Spurgeon said:

> Doth not all nature around me praise God? If I were silent, I should be an exception to the universe. Doth not the thunder praise Him as it rolls like drums in the march of the God of armies? Do not the mountains praise Him when the woods upon their summits wave in adoration? Does not the lightning write His name in letters of fire? Hath not the whole earth a voice? And shall I, can I, silent be?

I have long been a reader of Hal Borland, who, in his *Hill Country Harvest* and other writings, has the power to lead us along familiar roads into nature's beauty with a sensitivity that opens up whole new areas of meaning:

There are two times in the year when any person with a grain of sense, or sensitivity, can't stay indoors. One is in the spring, usually late April, when the outdoor world is on tip-toe, ready to burst into spring. That is the time when one walking along a country road or taking his time across an open meadow and along the edge of a woodland is privileged to participate in a kind of annual genesis. The other time is right after the first hard frost.

The color hasn't yet vanished, but a good deal of it is down out of the treetops. Quite a few maples and most of the oaks on my own mountainside are still full of leaves, but when I walk there I am ankle-deep in crisp gold and crimson. The roadsides are scuffing, and every breeze is full of leaves, it seems. If I pause beside a clump of sumac I am sure to be showered with color, for the sumac leaves are so loose that even my own breath will bring a few floating down. And when I stand beneath a red oak I can't believe there are so many leaves still on the tree because the ground seems to be covered with them. Which proves only that even an oak, which hasn't as many leaves as a maple the same size, has more leaves than I could count in a week.

I come to a tangle of tall weeds, mostly goldenrod and milkweed. The goldenrod is all brown stems and shriveled leaves, but the gray fluff of its seed plumes is like mist, riding every breath of air. And the milkweeds are a golden beauty, the leaves startlingly yellow, yellower than willow leaves. The pods, still gray-green, are already spilling their silken contents, and when the breeze passes it takes on the shimmer of milkweed floss.

At the roadside stands a tree that I knew in boyhood as a box elder. There's not a leaf left on it, but its twigs are loaded with brown tassels of seed, keys like those of the sugar maples in front of my house. This tree, of course, is one of the maple family, the ash-leaved maple; the keys prove it, and if there were further doubt one could tap it in early spring and make syrup from its sap. Just beyond is a barberry bush, its leaves deep purple, its berries brilliant scarlet. It stands in a fencerow, obviously planted there by the birds, as are most of the barberries that grow at the roadside. And the birds busy at this bush right now will plant still more barberries along other fencerows. Just as they have planted that golden tuft of asparagus that shines in the sunlight. I never notice how much asparagus grows wild until autumn, when the fine-cut fern foliage turns that unmistakable golden yellow, twinkling with ripe red berries.

Wild grape leaves are a rich tan. I have to stop and pluck one and feel its texture, which is almost exactly like that of a paper napkin. And while I am standing there I wonder which birds ate all the berries from the big, red-stemmed pokeweed. There's not one berry left, nothing but the wine-red splay of empty stems where the purple-black berries hung in a loose panicle two weeks ago. Those berries are mildly poisonous to people, but apparently the birds have no trouble digesting them. Glancing at the wild grape vine again I look for bunches of fruit, see only the empty stems and remember the October evening when I found a possum in a tangle of wild grape vines, stained with their juice from black nose tip to his very paws. Possums like those little grapes. So do foxes, though I never caught a fox as red-handed as I did that possum.

The asters are looking rather sad, though here and there I find a few big purples that evidently opened after the night of hard frost. They are particularly gay looking, and their golden centers look almost orange. And here is a bunch of bouncing Bet, still blooming bravely though its leaves are rather forlorn. But when I look up the hillside I see a stand of Christmas fern, its fronds as lively and green as they were in July. This fern pays little heed to the weather, though its cousins are brown as oak leaves, crisp as corn flakes.

A small flock of flickers comes swooping across the pasture, and as they go past I see the white rump patches. They won't be here much longer. As I follow their flight I know that they, too, are seeing the distant horizon as neither they nor I have seen it since last April. There it is, in plain sight through the bare branches of the trees, and those few trees still in leaf only make the new openness more noticeable.

The world has new dimensions now. It has broadened beyond summer belief. It summons the flickers to migration, and it summons me to reach and travel at least with my mind and my imagination. Valleys broaden now, and hilltops are out in the open. This is a world complete for another season, and if I do not go out and see it I am without understanding of creation itself.

Perhaps the greatest naturalist in American history was that lover of nature and teacher of its wise and healing secrets. John Burroughs writes:

If I were to name the three most precious resources of life, I should say books, friends, and nature; and the greatest of these, at least the most constant and always at hand, is nature. Nature we have always with us, an inexhaustible storehouse of that which moves the heart, appeals to the mind, and fires the imagination—health to the body, a stimulus to the intellect, and joy to the soul. To the scientist, nature is a storehouse of facts, laws, processes; to the artist she is a storehouse of pictures; to the poet she is a storehouse of images, fancies, a source of inspiration; to the moralist she is a storehouse of precepts and parables; to all she may be a source of knowledge and joy.

And John Kendrick Bangs, who evidently tried to convince someone of the presence of God, gives us a rather thoughtful poem:

BLIND

"Show me your God!" the doubter
cries.
I point him to the smiling skies;
I show him all the woodland greens;

> I show him peaceful sylvan scenes;
> I show him winter snows and frost;
> I show him waters tempest-tossed;
> I show him hills rock-ribbed and
>   strong;
> I bid him hear the thrush's song;
> I show him flowers in the close—
> The lily, violet, and rose;
> I show him rivers, babbling streams;
> I show him youthful hopes and dreams;
> I show him maids with eager hearts;
> I show him toilers in the marts;
> I show him stars, the moon, the sun;
> I show him deeds of kindness done;
> I show him joy; I show him care;
> And still he holds his doubting air,
> And faithless goes his way, for he
> Is blind of soul, and cannot see!

But Emerson, with his usual sensitivity and depth of insight, saw God everywhere in the beauty of the world and it became a blessing to him:

> Never lose an opportunity of seeing anything that is beautiful; for beauty is God's handwriting—a wayside sacrament. Welcome it in every fair face, in every fair sky, in every fair flower, and thank God for it as a cup of blessing.

A world of joyousness and enthusiasm, of delight and wonder is about us on every hand, but, unhappily, even the most amazing wonders can become commonplace through constancy of repetition. As Henry Wadsworth Longfellow says:

> If spring came but once in a century instead of once a year, or burst forth with the sound of an earthquake and not in silence, what wonder and expectation there would be in all hearts to behold the miraculous change.

An unknown author describes what we may find in this glorious God's world and our world to make us happy and surcharge us with enthusiasm for life:

THE DAWN

One morn I rose and looked upon the world.
"Have I been blind until this hour?" I said.
On every trembling leaf the sun had spread,
And was like golden tapestry unfurled;
And as the moments passed more light was hurled
Upon the drinking earth athirst for light;
And I, beholding all this wondrous sight,
Cried out aloud, "O God, I love Thy world!"
And since that waking, often I drink deep
The joy of dawn, and peace abides with me;
And though I know that I again shall see
Dark fear with withered hand approach my sleep,
More sure am I when lonely night shall flee,
At dawn the sun will bring good cheer to me.

Admiral Richard E. Byrd, in the frozen world of the South Pole listening to the vast and impalpable silence, found peace and God in the frigid twilight:

I paused to listen to the silence. My breath, crystallized as it passed my cheeks, drifted on a breeze gentler than a whisper. The wind vane pointed toward the South Pole. Presently the wind cups ceased their gentle turning as the cold killed the breeze. My frozen breath hung like a cloud overhead.

The day was dying, the night was being born—but with great peace. Here were the imponderable processes and forces of the cosmos, harmonious and soundless. Harmony, that was it! That was what came out of the silence—a gentle rhythm, the strain of a perfect chord, the music of the spheres, perhaps.

It was enough to catch that rhythm, momentarily to be myself a part of it. In that instant I could feel no doubt of man's oneness with the universe. The conviction came that that rhythm was too orderly, too harmonious, too perfect to be a product of blind chance—that, therefore, there must be purpose in the whole and that man was part of that whole and not an accidental offshoot. It was a feeling that transcended reason; that went to the heart of man's despair and found it groundless. The universe was a cosmos, not a chaos; man was as rightfully a part of that cosmos as were the day and night.

Charles A. Lindbergh, always a seeker after peace, found it alone one time especially. It was on his immortal and fabulous flight in the *Spirit of St. Louis:*

It's hard to be an agnostic up here in the *Spirit of St. Louis,* aware of the frailty of man's devices, a part of the universe between its earth and stars. If one dies, all this goes on existing in a plan so perfectly balanced, so wonderfully simple, so incredibly complex that it's far beyond our comprehension— worlds and moons revolving; planets orbiting on suns; suns flung with apparent recklessness through space. There's the infinite magnitude of the universe; there's the infinite detail of its matter—the outer star, the inner atom. And man conscious of it all—a worldly audience to what if not to God?

Jesus was the greatest intellectual who ever lived. He cut through all philosophizing by asking, "You want to be happy? Then love people and trust them."

I am enthusiastic about people. One of the happiest places I ever visited is one that used to be called a Reform School for Boys. (Now they have better names for such schools.) But no one visiting there would have thought it had anything to do with delinquent boys. It might have been Hotchkiss, Taft, Deerfield, Groton—any preparatory school. Living in a cottage system, the boys were fine, radiant-looking, manly and polite.

The school was established by Floyd Starr, who got the idea for it when he was four years old. Some visitor in his home told about adopting fifty homeless boys. The story fascinated the little boy, and he told his mother he was going to adopt fifty boys when he grew up. They laughed at him, of course. But, in college, just before graduation, when a group was sitting around in the fraternity house telling each other what they were going to do after commencement, Starr said, "I am going to adopt fifty of the worst boys I can find. I am going to love them and trust them into becoming great men. I don't think there is such a thing as a bad boy." They laughed at him again and said it couldn't be done. But today his establishment is "Starr Commonwealth for Boys" in Michigan.

The courts of Michigan will give any boy brought in for committing a crime the opportunity of going to Floyd Starr's school if he wishes. These boys are adjudged bad boys. One of them, sent from New Jersey, had the reputation of being the worst boy in the state. It was claimed that nothing could be done with him. Nevertheless on my recent visit when I helped dedicate a chapel, I saw this "bad boy" from New Jersey going around snuffing out candles and dressed in ecclesiastical costume. His face was radiant.

"He is going to be an Episcopal minister," Mr. Starr explained. "I do not care what boys have done. I am only interested in what they are and what they are going to be. I never look at a case history.

He had one of these boys drive him one evening to a meeting fifty miles away. When they arrived, he gave the boy a five-dollar bill, told him to get his supper and come back and pick him up about nine o'clock. Right on the dot of nine the boy arrived and handed him the change from the bill.

On the way home the boy said, "Uncle Floyd, you trust me, don't you?"

"Certainly," Mr. Starr answered.

"Why do you?" the boy asked. "You're the first one who ever did."

"Bill," Mr. Starr explained, "I trust you because I love you and believe in you."

"But, Uncle Floyd," the boy persisted, "don't you know why they sent me to your school?"

"No, Bill," he said, "I haven't the slightest idea."

Then the boy told him. He had come home one night to find an ambulance in front of his house. His father, drunk, had stabbed his mother. They were taking her to the hospital; they didn't expect her to live.

"They were drunk and swearing all the time," the boy said. "My father is in state prison now. I joined up with a gang and got away with plenty for a long time. They sent me here for stealing cars. And tonight you let me have your own car."

Mr. Starr slipped an arm around the boy's shoulders. "You are never going to steal cars again," he said.

Once in a while you meet a man so Christlike that it moves you to the depths of your heart. Such a man is Starr. As someone remarked to me during my visit, "What makes this such a happy place is that Starr-dust gets all over you."

In some schools of this kind, rehabilitation is 34 percent. Starr's record is 94 percent. Psychiatrists have told him he is foolish not to read the case histories. I think his results justify his methods.

Doesn't it make you happy to hear me tell about this man and his work? If you want to be happy in an unhappy world, quit hating people; quit hating anybody. Just skip it. Go around loving people. Believe in them. Where all other books fail, the Bible keeps on going because it gives us the technique for happy living in an unhappy world. "In him was life; and the life was the light of men" (John 1:4). That is the avenue to the joyous and enthusiastic life.

It has been a habit of ours—of my wife, Ruth, and me—to go to the Swiss Alps for a time each year. Usually we have a writing assignment which we tell ourselves we can do best among the snowy peaks and high alpine meadows.

During this time, we work every morning until nearly noon, then go to the small symphony orchestra concerts in the village. They always play the great and inspiring masterpieces. Then we set out onto the mountain paths winding through the valleys and rising among the cliffs, along surging and foaming streams that dash swiftly down to the strong flowing rivers below. All through the summer afternoons we walk six to eight miles, until the shadows begin to lengthen. Then we return to our hotel and soak in a hot bath before dinner, and then early to bed.

For years this has been part of our annual program of work and renewal. Always it has been a source of inexpressible joy and enthusiasm for this glorious world of beauty and for the even greater beauty of the people we have known. It all seemed to be perfectly summed up one Sunday at evensong in the little chapel by the lake shore where, in the German language, the congregation was singing

a hymn long known to us, one which united the beauty of nature and
of man in the creative harmony of Almighty God:

FOR THE BEAUTY OF THE EARTH

For the beauty of the earth,
    For the beauty of the skies,
For the love which from our birth
    Over and around us lies,
Lord of all, to Thee we raise
This our hymn of grateful praise.

For the beauty of each hour
    Of the day and of the night,
Hill and vale, and tree and flower,
    Sun and moon, and stars of light,
Lord of all, to Thee we raise
This our hymn of grateful praise.

For the joy of ear and eye,
    For the heart and mind's delight,
For the mystic harmony
    Linking sense to sound and sight,
Lord of all, to Thee we raise
This our hymn of grateful praise.

For the joy of human love,
    Brother, sister, parent, child,
Friends on earth, and friends above,
    For all gentle thoughts and mild,
Lord of all, to Thee we raise
This our hymn of grateful praise.

For each perfect gift of Thine,
    To our race so freely given,
Graces human and divine,
    Flowers of earth, and buds of heaven,
Lord of all, to Thee we raise
This our hymn of grateful praise.

FOLLIOTT SANDFORD PIERPOINT

As the words of the old hymn of praise wafted out that evening over the sweet-scented meadows and seemed to flow in melody up the nearby mountainsides, we were filled with an indescribable love of all things and all people and with an overwhelming love of life itself. I found myself thinking of some words of Dostoyevsky, one of my favorite writers, which later I looked up again and give you here:

> Love all God's creation, the whole and every grain of sand in it. Love every leaf, every ray of God's light. Love the animals, love the plants, love everything. If you love everything, you will perceive the divine mystery in things. Once you perceive it, you will begin to comprehend it better every day. And you will come at last to love the whole world with an all-embracing love.

And when one heeds that injunction, the result will be a love of the world which will manifest itself in a new and sensitized love of life itself. This in turn will activate joy and enthusiasm in full measure. Such joy, perhaps, as that which is described by John Kendrick Bangs:

TODAY

Today, whatever may annoy,
The word for me is Joy, just simple joy:
The joy of life;
The joy of children and of wife;
The joy of bright, blue skies;
The joy of rain; the glad surprise
Of twinkling stars that shine at night;
The joy of winged things upon their flight;
The joy of noonday, and the tried
True joyousness of eventide;
The joy of labor, and of mirth;
The joy of air, and sea, and earth—
The countless joys that ever flow from Him
Whose vast beneficence doth dim
The lustrous light of day,
And lavish gifts divine upon our way.

Whate'er there be of Sorrow
I'll put off till Tomorrow,
And when Tomorrow comes, why then
'Twill be Today and Joy again!

But some respond dolefully to these positive attitudes, objecting that neither joy nor enthusiasm nor excitement nor delight are possible when adversity stalks life; when one is ill or weak or blind or afflicted with multiple woes. But the great Helen Keller did not allow her handicaps to keep joy away, as she tells us exultantly:

IN THE GARDEN OF THE LORD

The word of God came unto me,
Sitting alone among the multitudes;
And my blind eyes were touched with light,
And there was laid upon my lips a flame of fire.

I laugh and shout for life is good,
Though my feet are set in silent ways.
In merry mood I leave the crowd
To walk in my garden. Even as I walk
I gather fruits and flowers in my hands,
And with joyful heart I bless the sun
That kindles all the place with radiant life.
I run with playful winds that blow the scent
Of rose and jasmine in eddying whirls.

At last I come where tall lilies grow,
Lifting their faces like white saints to God.
While the lilies pray, I kneel upon the ground:
I have strayed into the holy temple of the Lord.

Some of life's best lessons are taught by things like trees, for example. At our place on Quaker Hill in Pawling, New York, which we call The Hill Farm, our family has learned much from wise old Mother Nature.

One thing is how trees handle storms. They move with the wind as it mounts in intensity, not with fear of the tempest nor by resisting it. They just bend with it, and as the tumult and force of a line storm gale increases, the boiling of the leaves of the gigantic old maples seems as if the tree is laughing with glee in the knowledge that it can ride out the storm, which it always seems to do. Next morning the storm is over and the sun is out. The ground may be strewn with leaves and twigs and perhaps a branch or two, which was about to be discarded by the tree anyway. But the tree still stands and actually is stronger than ever, having wrestled with and overcome another storm in its long life.

This tells us something about how we human beings can also ride out our storms in life. Bend with the wind. Lean against it. Laugh with it. Rejoice in struggle. It grows you strong.

I like the way pine trees handle a big snowfall. The accumulating snows lie heavy on the supple branches, but those branches seldom break. They just yield gracefully to the extra weight of the snow. And in due course the pine tree's friends, the wind and the sun, either blow it off or melt it, and then the branches slowly—never hurriedly—come back to normal position—which isn't a bad technique for a person to learn!

And then I cannot fail to mention our cherished old apple tree. It must be at least a hundred years old. Once it was quite large for its species; perhaps three feet thick, with a wide spread of branches. But now the trunk has been reduced to a width of no more than three or four inches, and at its center is a large hole two feet long and eight inches wide. But even this reduced trunk sturdily holds up the spread of branches. The tree is in a spot protected from the main force of winds, but it gets its share of the wind, rain, ice and snow in the changing seasons.

I marvel at this tree, for it is old and reduced in structure, its youth and the vigor of its prime gone. But it does not know that it is old and weakened. Every springtime it puts out its blossoms, as it always has done, and as a matter of fact it seems to outdo the blossom business, for its branches are overwhelmingly full of pinkish-white blooms, and it is a sight to behold.

Then come the apples. We never have sprayed this old tree, but even so the fruit is crisp and juicy, apart from a few worms and rough spots. Ruth makes delicious applesauce from them. The tree demonstrates a powerful loyalty to its purpose, which is of course to put out leaves in the spring, to blossom and to produce apples in the fall; and it just continues, with fidelity to its purpose in being, to do that despite age and decrepitude. So every year, spring and fall, I go and stand beneath its spreading branches and reverently salute the old tree as my teacher, saying to it, "Dear old apple tree, I am going to keep on doing my job and I hope to do it as well as you do yours."

As long as I live and own the place, that tree will never be cut down, unless some winter gale proves too strong for it. Then I will sadly yield it to time and the elements, but cherish it forever in memory.

Henry David Thoreau, one of that small coterie of thinkers who really set the tone of early America, writes of snowflakes, and that, too, is a big part of the New England-New York State country heritage:

SWEEPINGS OF HEAVEN'S FLOOR

Nature is full of genius, full of the divinity, so that not a snowflake escapes its fashioning hand. Nothing is cheap and coarse, neither dewdrops nor snowflakes.

Myriads of these little disks, so beautiful to the most prying eyes, are whirled down on every traveler's coat, the observant and the unobservant, on the restless squirrel's fur, on the far-stretching fields and forests, the wooded dells and mountain tops.

Far, far away from the haunts of men, they roll down some little slope, fall over and come to their bearings, and melt or lose their beauty in the mass, ready anon to swell some little rill with their contribution, and so, at last, the universal ocean from which they came. There they lie, like the wreck of chariot wheels after a battle in the sky.

Meanwhile the meadow mouse shoves them aside in his gallery, the school boy casts them in his snowball, or the woodman's sled glides smoothly over them, these glorious spangles, these sweepings of heaven's floor.

And they all sing, melting as they sing, of the mysteries of the number six, six, six, six.

He takes up the water of the sea in His hand, leaving the salt; He dispenses it in mist through the sky, He re-collects

and sprinkles it like grain in six-rayed stars over the earth,
there to lie till it dissolves in bonds again.

And the Psalmist, with consummate descriptive skill, exalts the
mighty power of God the Creator:

He formed the mountains by his mighty strength. He
quiets the raging oceans and all the world's clamor. In the far-
thest corners of the earth the glorious acts of God shall startle
everyone. The dawn and sunset shout for joy! He waters the
earth to make it fertile. The rivers of God will not run dry! He
prepares the earth for his people and sends them rich harvests
of grain. He waters the furrows with abundant rain. Showers
soften the earth, melting the clods and causing seeds to sprout
across the land. Then he crowns it all with green, lush pas-
tures in the wilderness; hillsides blossom with joy. The pas-
tures are filled with flocks of sheep, and the valleys are car-
peted with grain. All the world shouts with joy, and sings.
Psalms 65:6–13, TLB

From Tay Thomas (Mrs. Lowell Thomas, Jr.) comes a vivid description of the beauty of Alaska in autumn, from her book *Only in
Alaska:*

One doesn't mind the loss of the flowers, however, when
the trees and undergrowth begin to change their color. Accustomed as I was to the brilliance of New England falls, the
bright, intense splash of colors here still leaves me breathless.
Autumn is far too brief in the Far North—it lasts two or three
weeks at the most—but nature seems determined to make up
for the brevity by supplying the hues of yellows and reds in
double strength. The small wild dogwood, lingonberry, and
strawberry plants closest to the ground turn a deep red first,
followed by the taller fireweed, wild rose, wild red currant,
and rusty menziesia. Amid this bright red wild growth, the
large leaves of the devil's-club turn a vivid yellow. Then the
leaves of the birch and aspen become such a rich and brilliant
gold that on clear days even the most unartistic person is

highly tempted to reach for a paintbrush and try to capture the scene. And it isn't just the yellows and reds of the leaves—the waters of the lakes and the inlet turn an extra-deep blue, the birch bark seems whiter, and the mountains take on soft, gentle hues of red, beneath violet-colored peaks.

The blessings of life and the natural world confer upon the person of faith the healing, strengthening and hope needed to carry on valiantly day by day. As Fred Bauer tells us:

> FOR QUIET I LIKE UNSPEAKING TREES
> for quiet I like unspeaking trees
> for cares a spirited mountain walk
> for fulfillment someone to please
> for laughter hearing children talk
>
> for reassurance a hand to hold
> for strength the persevering sea
> for understanding a friendship old
> for hope I turn to Thee

Charles A. Lindbergh, alone amidst the silent vastness of skies over the Atlantic, found the peace and greatness of God in moon flow:

I'd almost forgotten the moon. Now, like a neglected ally, it's coming to my aid. Every minute will bring improving sight. As the moon climbs higher in the sky, its light will brighten, until finally it ushers in the sun. The stars ahead are already fading. The time is 10:20. There have been only two hours of solid darkness.

Gradually, as light improves, the night's black masses turn into a realm of form and texture. Silhouettes give way to shadings. Clouds open their secret details to the eyes. In the moon's reflected light, they seem more akin to it than to the earth over which they hover. They form a perfect setting for that strange foreign surface one sees through a telescope trained on the satellite of the world. Formations of the moon, they are—volcanoes and flat plateaus; great towers and bottomless pits; crevasses and canyons; ledges no earthly mountains ever knew—reality combined with the fantasy of a dream. There are shapes like growths of coral on the bed of a tropical sea, or the grotesque canyons of sandstone and lava at the edge of Arizona deserts—first black, then gray, now greenish hue in cold, mystical light.

I weave in and out, eastward, toward Europe, hidden away in my plane's tiny cockpit, submerged, alone, in the magnitude of this weird, unhuman space, venturing where man has never been, irretrievably launched on a flight through this sacred garden of the sky, this inner shrine of higher spirits. Am I myself a living, breathing, earth-bound body, or is this a dream of death I'm passing through? Am I alive, or am I really dead, a spirit in a spirit world? Am I actually in a plane boring through the air, over the Atlantic, toward Paris, or have I crashed on some worldly mountain, and is this the afterlife?

For a moment the clouds give way, and the moon itself peers through a tremendous valley, flooding unearthly bluffs with its unearthly light, screening the eastern stars with its nearer, brighter glow, assuming mastery of the sky by night as does the sun by day.

Far ahead, a higher cloud layer is forming, thousands of feet above my level—glowing, horizontal strips, supported by thick pillars from the mass below—sculptured columns and arches to a temple of the moon. Has the sky opened only to close again? Will they finally merge, these clouds, to form one great mass of opaque air? Must I still turn back? *Can* I still turn back, or have I been lured to this forbidden temple to find all doors have closed? North, south, and west, clouds rise and tower; only the lighted corridors ahead are clear.

I've been tunneling by instruments through a tremendous cumulus mass. As I break out, a glaring valley lies across my path, miles in width, extending north and south as far as I can see. The sky is blue-white above, and the blinding fire of the sun itself has burst over the ridge ahead. I nose the *Spirit of St. Louis* down, losing altitude slowly, two hundred feet or so a minute. At eight thousand feet, I level out, plumbing with my eyes the depth of each chasm I pass over. In the bottom of one of them, I see it, like a rare stone perceived among countless pebbles at your feet—a darker, deeper shade, a different texture—the ocean! Its surface is splotched with white and covered with ripples. Ripples from eight thousand feet! That means a heavy sea.

It's one of those moments when all the senses rise together, and realization snaps so acute and clear that seconds impress themselves with the strength of years on memory. It forms a picture with colors that will hold and lines that will stay sharp throughout the rest of life—the broad, sun-dazzled valley in the sky; the funnel's billowing walls; and deep down below, the hard, blue-gray scales of the ocean.

Emerson would have understood the deep-level feelings of Lindbergh:

> The man who has seen the rising moon break out of the clouds at midnight has been present like an archangel at the creation of light and of the world.

Taken all in all, the glory and wonder of this planet upon which we are permitted to live for a time brings us finally to sing with Maltbie D. Babcock that "This Is My Father's World":

> This is my Father's world,
> And to my listening ears,
> All nature sings, and round me rings
> The music of the spheres.
> This is my Father's world:
> I rest me in the thought
> Of rocks and trees, of skies and seas;
> His hand the wonders wrought.
>
> This is my Father's world,
> The birds their carols raise,
> The morning light, the lily white,
> Declare their Maker's praise.

This is my Father's world:
He shines in all that's fair;
In the rustling grass I hear Him pass,
He speaks to me everywhere.

This is my Father's world,
O! let me ne'er forget
That though the wrong seems oft so strong,
God is the Ruler yet.
This is my Father's world:
The battle is not done;
Jesus who died shall be satisfied,
And earth and heaven be one.

10

Dare to Be Happy

THERE IS AN OLD ANONYMOUS POEM which I have always liked. In a down-to-earth sort of way it describes the happiness and zest for life which comes when one just lives in a loving and caring manner:

FELLOWSHIP

When a feller hasn't got a cent
And is feelin' kind of blue,
And the clouds hang thick and dark
And won't let the sunshine thro',
It's a great thing, oh my brethren,
For a feller just to lay
His hand upon your shoulder in a friendly sort o' way.

It makes a man feel queerish,
It makes the tear-drops start.
And you kind o' feel a flutter
In the region of your heart.
You can't look up and meet his eye,
You don't know what to say
When a hand is on your shoulder in a friendly sort o' way.

Oh this world's a curious compound
With its honey and its gall;
Its cares and bitter crosses,
But a good world after all.
And a good God must have made it,
Leastwise that is what I say,
When a hand is on your shoulder in a friendly sort o' way.

Feeling toward other people in the way that poem suggests goes a long way toward giving one a sense of worth, a feeling that life is meaningful. Charles Dickens says it well:

No one is useless in the world who lightens the burden of it for anyone else.

And Leo Tolstoy says:

Joy can be real only if people look upon their life as a service, and have a definite object in life outside themselves and their personal happiness.

So it would appear that to have real joy and enthusiasm one must drop or reduce self-emphasis and become genuinely outgoing; develop the attitude of good will or perhaps make it even stronger— that of love for all kinds of people. People need love, and the person who wholeheartedly gives love to them is loved by them and that induces a deep and genuine happiness all around. I knew a famous humorist of my boyhood days who was also a man with a big heart. He was a happy man whose joy and excitement for life derived from his love of people. He wrote this poem called "Need of Loving":

Folk need a lot of loving in the morning;
    The day is all before, with cares beset—
The cares we know, and they that give no warning;
    For love is God's own antidote for fret.

Folk need a heap of loving at the noontime—
    In the battle lull, the moment snatched from strife—
Halfway between the waking and the croontime,
    While bickering and worriment are rife.

Folk hunger so for loving at the nighttime,
    When wearily they take them home to rest—
At slumber song and turning-out-the-light time—
    Of all the times for loving, that's the best.

Folk want a lot of loving every minute—
    The sympathy of others and their smile!

Till life's end, from the moment they begin it,
Folks need a lot of loving all the while.

STRICKLAND GILLILAN

And I have personal memories of Edwin Markham in his latter years, a white-haired genial giant with whom I once spent a never-to-be-forgotten evening. Asked which of his poems he valued the highest, he answered, "How can you choose between your own children?" He did voice the opinion that his four lines called "Outwitted" might have lasting qualities because love lasts. And I had the feeling that the really deep joy of this great American poet stemmed in large measure from the genuine outgoing love the man had for his fellows:

He drew a circle that shut me out—
Heretic, rebel, a thing to flout.
But Love and I had the wit to win:
We drew a circle that took him in!

Many people are lonely in this world, and that, too, is a painful experience. Anyone who helps another person out of loneliness will make two persons joyful: the lonely one and the one who helps. As John Oxenham says:

Are you lonely, O my brother?
Share your little with another!
Stretch your hand to one unfriended,
And your loneliness is ended.

So deep and meaningful is the joy and the enthusiasm that is born in one's mind and heart by human love and helpfulness that it has the power to motivate for a lifetime.

A physician well on in years told me how he became a doctor. His story was so wonderful that I never forgot it. He told me that, as a small boy, he lived with his parents in Kansas, in a district where, in wintertime, the countryside often lay under deep drifted snow and there would be difficulty getting in and out between town and his family's farm.

One winter when he was about seven years old, his little sister got sick, ran a high fever, became delirious. By the time his father got a message over the well-nigh impassable roads to the doctor, and the doctor finally arrived, with horse and buggy breaking through the snow, the little girl was sick unto death. The doctor remained for twenty-four hours until the crisis was passed. The whole household was in anguish. No one had a minute's sleep.

Finally the little boy saw the doctor walk across the room and put his hands on the shoulders of his father and mother, and heard him say to them, "By the grace of God, I am happy to tell you that little Mary will get well." The boy, from where he stood crouching behind a chair, could see his parents' faces in that moment. He had never seen them so beautiful, so lighted up, so wonderfully happy. They had been made that way by what the doctor had said to them.

"Right in that moment," my friend concluded, "I decided I was going to be a doctor, so I could say things like that to people that would bring that light to their eyes, that joy to their faces."

You don't have to be a doctor to say or do that which puts light in a human eye and joy on a human face. Simply practice Jesus' commandment that we love one another. Go out and do something for somebody. These are the things that make happy people happy. "If ye know these things, happy are ye if ye do them" (John 13:17). Here is the one never-failing source of the joy and enthusiasm we are talking about throughout this book.

No wonder that Christianity, which teaches the way to happy life, emphasizes and underscores love. Three great words there are— *faith, hope, love;* but the greatest of the three greatest words in the English language, or, indeed, any language, is *love.* And "Love never fails . . ." (1 Corinthians 13:8, NKJV).

Saint John says:

Greater love hath no man than this, that a man lay down his life for his friends.

John 15:13

And this commandment have we from him, That he who loveth God love his brother also.

1 John 4:21

And in Galatians we read:

> Bear ye one another's burdens, and so fulfil the law of
> Christ.

Galatians 6:2

And those who pass on kindness and love as they journey through
this life are carrying out the rules for the good and happy life, which
are set like jewels in the Scriptures. This poem by Henry Burton will
encourage us to pass our joy on:

PASS IT ON

Have you had a kindness shown?
    Pass it on.
'Twas not given for thee alone,
    Pass it on.
Let it travel down the years,
Let it wipe another's tears,
'Till in heav'n the deed appears—
    Pass it on.

Did you hear the loving word?
    Pass it on.
Like the singing of a bird?
    Pass it on.
Let its music live and grow
Let it cheer another's woe;
You have reaped what others sow—
    Pass it on.

'Twas the sunshine of a smile—
    Pass it on.
Staying but a little while!
    Pass it on.
April beam a little thing,
Still it wakes the flowers of spring,
Makes the silent birds to sing—
    Pass it on.

One of the happy things you can do for someone else and so bring new joy and enthusiasm to yourself is to help that person face a devastating experience and overcome it. There is a middle-aged businessman who gives me renewed zest every time I see him, for he never fails to remind me of the day he "really hit bottom" in his career, as he expresses it. He credits me with helping him to recover from a "blow that nearly finished me off." I really did not do all that much for him that day except that I cared, and happened to have at hand a little story full of human wisdom that grabbed his mind. Anyway, it turned him from failure to success.

I talked with a young man who had been fired from a good position for making a serious mistake. A bit strange, I thought, for a company to throw out a young fellow for one mistake. I knew a famous employer who would allow at least two mistakes. Around his plant were signs reading HE WHO STUMBLES TWICE ON THE SAME STONE DESERVES TO BREAK HIS OWN NECK.

I pointed out to the dejected young fellow that mistakes could originate from an error pattern in one's thinking, or from inexperience, or from carelessness. But in any event you should derive what know-how the experience contained and then don't let it throw you. Turn your back on it; look to the future; try again. I happened to have on my desk at the time an editorial from the Toledo *Blade* written by my old friend, Grove Patterson, a famous newspaper editor, for whom I once worked on a Detroit paper. It was titled "Water Under the Bridge." I read it to the crushed young man:

A boy a long time ago leaned against the railing of a bridge and watched the current of the river below. A log, a bit of driftwood, a chip floated past. Again the surface of the river was smooth. But always, as it had for a hundred, perhaps a thousand, perhaps even a million years, the water slipped by under the bridge. Sometimes the current went more swiftly and again quite slowly, but always the river flowed on under the bridge.

Watching the river that day, the boy made a discovery. It was not the discovery of a material thing, something he might put his hand upon. He could not even see it. He had discovered an idea. Quite suddenly, and yet quietly, he knew that everything in his life would some day pass under the bridge and be gone like the water.

The boy came to like those words *water under the bridge*. All his life thereafter the idea served him well and carried him through. Although there were days and ways that were dark and not easy, always when he had made a mistake that couldn't be helped, or lost something that could never come again, the boy, now a man, said, "It's water under the bridge."

And he didn't worry unduly about his mistakes after that and he certainly didn't let them get him down, because it was *water under the bridge*.

The young man sat without a word. Then he stood up. I had a feeling the editorial had registered. "Okay," he said, "I get it. It's water under the bridge. I'll try again." And he did all right, because he learned the very great truth that no failure ever need be final. Because you failed, made a mistake, acted stupidly does not indicate lack of brains or ability. It's just that now and then anyone can stumble or even take a bad fall. But that does not mean that you are not all right yourself. Just pick yourself up mentally. Say, "Okay, that happened, but now it has passed. I'll turn my back on all of it and look confidently to the future." Keep on believing in yourself. Have confidence.

The young man made more mistakes, of course, as we all do, but thereafter he knew how to handle them, and the number and importance of his errors averaged very low. It is not at all strange that when we meet at rare intervals we are both happy and enthusiastic, as is bound to be the case between the helped and the helper.

The famous poet Emily Dickinson has something important to say on this matter of helping people:

IF I CAN STOP ONE HEART FROM BREAKING

> If I can stop one heart from breaking,
> I shall not live in vain;
> If I can ease one life the aching,
> Or cool one pain,
> Or help one fainting robin

Unto his nest again,
I shall not live in vain.

And so does the notable writer Henry Drummond:

THE RETURN

Instead of allowing yourself to be unhappy, just let your love grow as God wants it to grow. Seek goodness in others. Love more persons more. Love them more impersonally, more unselfishly, without thought of return. The return, never fear, will take care of itself.

George Eliot issues a warning that no day should be allowed to pass except we do something to help at least one person, that is, if we expect to live a happy life:

COUNT THAT DAY LOST

If you sit down at set of sun
And count the acts that you have done,
   And counting find
One self-denying deed, one word
That eased the heart of him who heard;
   One glance most kind,
That fell like sunshine where it went—
Then you may count that day well spent.

But if, through all the livelong day,
You've cheered no heart, by yea or nay—
   If, through it all
You've nothing done that you can trace
That brought the sunshine to one face—
   No act most small
That helped some soul and nothing cost—
Then count that day as worse than lost.

And, to further impress this important point upon our minds— that we do not forget to do the simple, nice and kindly things, I give you a poem by Margaret E. Sangster:

THE SIN OF OMISSION

It isn't the thing you do;
    It's the thing you leave undone,
Which gives you a bit of heartache
    At the setting of the sun.

The tender word forgotten,
    The letter you did not write,
The flower you might have sent,
    Are your haunting ghosts at night.

The stone you might have lifted
    Out of a brother's way,
The bit of heartsome counsel
    You were hurried too much to say;

The loving touch of the hand,
    The gentle and winsome tone,
That you had no time or thought for
    With troubles enough of your own.

The little acts of kindness,
    So easily out of mind;
Those chances to be helpful
    Which everyone may find—

No, it's not the thing you do,
    It's the thing you leave undone,
Which gives you the bit of heartache
    At the setting of the sun.

My Christmas Eve discovery took place in Brooklyn, New York. I was feeling happy because things were going well with my church. As a young bachelor minister I had just had a fine visit with some friends and was saying good-bye to them on their front steps.

All around us up and down the street houses were decorated in honor of Christ's birthday. Suddenly a pair of wreaths on the house across the street caught my eye. One had the traditional red bow, bright and gay. But the ribbon on the other was a somber black—the symbol of a death in the family, a funeral wreath. It was the custom at that time and place to hang such wreaths outside a house of mourning.

Something about that unexpected juxtaposition of joy and sorrow made a strange and moving impression on me. I asked my host about it. He said that a young couple with small children lived in the house but he did not know them. They were new in the neighborhood.

I said good night and walked down the street. But before I had gone far, something made me turn back. I did not know those people either. But it was Christmas Eve, and if there was joy or suffering to be shared, my calling was to share it.

Hesitantly I went up to the door and rang the bell. A tall young man opened it and spoke pleasantly to me. I told him that I was a minister whose church was in the neighborhood. I had seen the wreaths and wanted to offer my sympathy.

"Come in," he said quietly. "It's very kind of you to come."

The house seemed very still. In the living room a wood fire was burning. In the center of the room was a small casket. In it reposed the body of a little girl about six years old. Over the years in memory I can see her yet, lying there in a pretty white dress, ironed fresh and dainty. Nearby was an empty chair where the young man had been sitting, keeping watch beside the body of his child.

I was so moved that I could barely speak. *What a Christmas Eve*, I thought. Alone in a new neighborhood, no friends or relatives, a crushing loss. The young man seemed to read my thoughts. "It's all right," he said, as if he were reassuring me. "She's with the Lord, you know." His wife, he said, was upstairs with their two smaller children. He took me to meet her.

The young mother was reading to two small boys. She had a lovely face, sad yet serene. And suddenly I knew why this little family had been able to hang two wreaths on the door, one signifying life, the other death. They had been able to do it because they knew it was all one process, all part of God's wonderful and merciful and perfect plan for all of us. They had heard the great promise: ". . . because I live, ye shall live also" (John 14:19). They had heard it and they believed it. That was why they could move forward together with love and dignity, courage and acceptance.

The young couple asked if they could join my church. They did. We became good friends. Many years have passed since then, but not one has gone by without a Christmas card from some member of that family expressing love and gratitude.

But I am the one who is grateful.

I sometimes find myself thinking of an anonymous poem I like, for it speaks of the simple kindness we should be spreading:

> I SHALL NOT PASS THIS WAY AGAIN
> Through this toilsome world, alas!
> Once and only once I pass;
> If a kindness I may show,
> If a good deed I may do
> To a suffering fellow man,
> Let me do it while I can.
> No delay, for it is plain
> I shall not pass this way again.

The joy we derive and the enthusiasm we may develop by thinking of the neglected and the lonely cannot be minimized. And to receive this wonderful blessing is often all so simple. All we need do is make a telephone call or write a letter, and a chain of joyousness and gratitude is set in motion.

I once had a friend, a great big-hearted man, a college professor and minister, Dr. William L. Stidger. One Thanksgiving Day during a recession and hard times when his friends were grumbling about "nothing to be thankful for," Dr. Stidger got to thinking. And he wrote this piece:

> We were a group of friends in the midst of an after-dinner conversation. Because Thanksgiving was just around the corner and prosperity wasn't, we fell to talking about what we had to be thankful for. As I look back, it seems to me the conversation was rather cynical.
>
> One member of the group, a minister, described the outline for his sermon on the theme *Thankful for What, This Depression Year?* His approach was so negative that the rest of us began a barrage of criticism.
>
> "All right, I'm a realist and I intended to be honest about

it," he replied. "If you don't like what you call my negative approach to Thanksgiving, then give me something to talk about that is affirmative."

That started us to thinking about what we had to be thankful for. One of us said: "Well I, for one, am grateful to Mrs. Wendt, an old schoolteacher who thirty years ago in a little West Virginia town went out of her way to introduce me to Tennyson."

Then he launched into a colorful description of Mrs. Wendt, a lovely little old lady who had been his high school teacher and who evidently had made a deep impression on his life. She had gone out of her way to awaken his literary interest and develop his gifts for expression. His was a dramatic and vivid description of a simple and natural small-town schoolteacher who had taken her work seriously.

"And does this Mrs. Wendt know that she made that contribution to your life?" someone put in.

"I'm afraid that she doesn't. I have been careless and have never, in all of these years, told her either face-to-face or by letter."

"Then why don't you write her? It would make her happy if she is still living, and it might make you happier, too. The thing that most of us ought to do is to learn to develop the attitude of gratitude."

Now, all this is very poignant to me, because Mrs. Wendt was *my* teacher, and *I* was the fellow who hadn't written. That friend's challenge made me see that I had accepted something very precious and hadn't bothered to say thanks.

That very evening, I tried to atone. On the chance that Mrs. Wendt might still be living, I sat down and wrote her what I called a Thanksgiving letter. I reminded her that it was she who had introduced my young mind to Tennyson and Browning and others.

It took about a week for the Post Office Department to search for Mrs. Wendt with my letter. It was forwarded from town to town. Finally it reached her, and this is the note I had in return, handwritten in the feeble scrawl of an old woman. It began:

My dear Willie—

[That introduction itself was quite enough to warm my heart. Here was a man of fifty, fat and bald, addressed as "Willie." I had to smile over that, and then I read on:]

I remember well your enthusiasm for Tennyson and the Idylls of the King when I read them to you, for you were so beautifully responsive. My reward for telling you about Tennyson did not have to wait until your belated note of thanks came to me in my old age. I received my best reward in your eager response to the lyrical beauty and the idealism of Tennyson. I shall never forget the way you read aloud to me:

My strength is as the strength of ten/Because my heart is pure!

But, in spite of the fact that I got much of my reward at that time, I want you to know what your note meant to me. I am now an old lady in my eighties, living alone in a small room, cooking my own meals, lonely and seemingly like the last leaf of fall left behind; or, as the old song used to put it, "The last rose of summer."

You will be interested to know, Willie, that I taught school for fifty years and, in all that time, yours is the first note of appreciation I ever received. It came on a blue, cold morning, and it cheered my lonely old heart as nothing has cheered me in many years.

I wept over that simple, sincere note from my teacher of long ago. I read it to a dozen friends. One of them said: "I believe I'm going to write Miss Mary Scott a letter. She did something similar to that for my boyhood!"

That first Thanksgiving letter was so successful and satisfying that I made a list of people who had contributed something definite and lasting to my life and planned to write at least one Thanksgiving letter every day in November. On the list were my father and mother, my brother and sisters, my grammar-school, high-school, and college teachers, some fellow ministers, and friends who had come to my side in hours of trouble and had helped me to see light through darkness. There were more than a hundred names on the list, and I hadn't thanked one of them! I could hardly wait to write my second letter.

It went to a college friend named Louis Sherwin, now a Presbyterian minister in Chicago.

One day he had arrived at Moundsville, West Virginia. It was midsummer and I had recently been graduated from high school. I was lying in an old barrel-stave hammock, which I had made. He sat on the steps of our porch and talked to me about going to Allegheny College. I remembered that he talked enthusiastically about the football team, the beautiful campus, and the professors who did the teaching, of course.

Then and there I decided to go to his college, whereupon he dropped the matter and pulled out of his pocket a small leather-bound copy of Robert Louis Stevenson, read to me from it for half an hour and then, just as he departed, gave that book to me. I still have it.

There was a Thanksgiving letter for Louis, asking him if he remembered that hot summer afternoon and the gift he had left behind. And in a week I had his letter back. He was then in Oil City, Pennsylvania. The last line of his letter read: "I have not had such an easy time, Bill, and I cannot tell you how your letter has really helped me."

The next summer I received from Edinburgh, Scotland, a leather-bound copy of another Stevenson book from Stevenson's own city. Louis was so grateful for my letter of thanks that, while traveling through Scotland, he had thought of me again.

The list of Thanksgiving letters sent out that November numbered fifty. All but two brought answers immediately, and those two were returned by relatives with the information that the addressees were dead. Even those letters expressed thanks for the little bit of thoughtfulness.

For ten years, I have kept up this exciting game of writing Thanksgiving-month letters. I have a special file for answers, and I now have more than five hundred of the most beautiful letters anyone has ever received. I never dreamed the response would be so satisfying. I had merely thought of building up in myself an attitude of gratitude such as my friend suggested that night.

One of the most beautiful and touching letters came from the late Bishop William F. McDowell, in whose Washington home I had found some needed rest before a speaking engagement. Seeing that I was tired out, Mrs. McDowell put me to bed to rest, and I was so grateful for that motherly thoughtfulness that I never forgot it. And yet I had never written her a letter of thanks.

When I started in on my Thanksgiving letters I remembered her and, knowing that she was gone, I wrote my thank-you letter to the bishop, going over the memory and telling him all about it. I received this in response:

> My Dear Will:
>
> Your thanksgiving letter, as you called it, was so beautiful, so real, that as I sat reading it in my study the tears fell from my eyes, tears of gratitude. Then, before I realized what I was doing I arose from my chair, called her name and started to show it to her—for the moment forgetting that she was gone. You will never know how much your letter has warmed my spirit. I have been walking about in the glow of it all day long.

A Thanksgiving letter isn't much. Only a few lines are necessary, and a stamp to mail it. But the rewards are so great that eternity alone can estimate them. Even now, in dark moments of discouragement, I go over these responses to my Thanksgiving letters, and drive away any darkness by reading a few selected at random.

I often wondered where Bill Stidger got all that joy and that enthusiasm which were so characteristic of him. And this little story lets me in on his secret.

But some people actually seem afraid to be happy. Subconsciously they feel that something bad is going to happen. They may even believe it is not right to be joyful with so much suffering in the world.

But you hardly help the unhappy by acting unhappy yourself. By your happiness you can actually pick them up. And by a joyous, enthusiastic spirit you can get out there and make it a better world for everyone.

Perhaps all you need do to be happy is simply to smile and do simple good deeds and rejoice over the happiness of others. Like Charles Lamb, for example, who says:

> The greatest pleasure I know is to do a good action by stealth, and to have it found out by accident.

And Archibald Rutledge has a fine idea:

> One of the sanest, surest, and most generous joys of life comes from being happy over the good fortune of others.

And I like what Robert Louis Stevenson says:

> A happy man or woman is a radiant focus of good will, and their entrance into a room is as though another candle had been lighted.

My joyous friend Frank Bettger wrote:

> I have asked thousands of men and women in audiences all over the country for a pledge to smile, just for *thirty days*, their happiest smile at every living creature they see. Easily 75 per cent of the people in each audience willingly raised their hands. What has been the result? I quote from one letter received from a Knoxville, Tennessee, man. It is typical of several letters which have come to me:
>
> > My wife and I had just about agreed to separate. Of course, I thought she was entirely at fault. Within a few days after I began to put this idea into action, happiness was restored in my home. I then came to realize that I had been losing out in business because of a sullen, losing attitude. At the end of the day, I would go home and

take it out on my wife and children. It was all my fault, not my wife's at all. I am a totally different man from what I was a year ago. I'm happier because I've made others happy too. Now everybody greets me with a smile. In addition my business has shown surprising improvement.

This man was so excited about the results he got from smiling, that he kept writing me for years about it!

Just having enough love in your heart for people to get out there and help them, you will experience exquisite joy and live with enthusiasm and joyous excitement.

Read this story by Alexander Lake, a newspaper reporter, and you will have a heart full of joy and with it a greater respect for what people can be:

CHRISTMAS EVE MIRACLE

One Christmas Eve, when I was a police reporter on the Seattle *Post Intelligencer*, I was idling at my typewriter in the police station press room when an overwhelming impulse sent me hurrying to Pioneer Square, three blocks down the street, where I arrived just in time to knock a loaded revolver away from the head of a man about to shoot himself.

A cold drizzle was falling, and the gun slid across the glistening path and came to rest in the grass. The little park was deserted. For an unreal moment, I stared at the illuminated hands of a clock in the window of a restaurant across the street. They read five minutes past seven.

Three or four minutes ago, I'd been half-dozing in the warm, poorly ventilated reporters' room. Now here I was at the foot of Seattle's Skid Row with a man I'd just saved from death.

Whence had come the impulse that sent me out into the dreary night? What had directed me to the exact spot where a fellow human was about to blast himself into eternity? It seemed so fantastic that I wondered if I was dreaming. However, I didn't have time to think much about it for the man suddenly dropped to his knees and began fumbling in the wet grass for the gun.

I pushed him with my foot, and he sprawled on his face. I picked up the gun and slipped it into my coat pocket. Then I helped the man to his feet. He was blubbering.

"Snap out of it, fellow," I said. "I'm here to help you. Let's go across to that restaurant and get some hot soup, or something."

He didn't answer. I put my hand on his shoulder.

"For God's sake," he said, "go away. Leave me alone." Then he covered his face with his hands.

Rain was running down the back of my neck, and I pulled up my coat collar. "Come on, Jack. Snap out of it," I said.

He looked at me. "You know me?" he asked.

"No."

"You called me *Jack*."

"Okay, Jack. Let's go someplace where it's dry. Someplace where we can talk."

He shook his head. "I don't want to talk," he said. But he did want to talk, for words began pouring from him.

"I can't go on," he said. "I can't face them. They have no food. No Christmas presents. I'm tired and sick. I'm in hell."

"Who are they?" I said.

"My family. My wife and kids. I've walked these streets for six days with that stuff," he said, pointing to a square bundle lying on the walk. "Stuff to prevent windshields fogging," he explained. "I've been trying to sell it. Six days. Know how much I've made? Seventy-five cents."

"How about that soup now, Jack?" I said.

"Yes . . . Jack," he said bitterly. "Jack Bryan—Auto Accessories. Know what? The constable locked the doors of my business last week. Didn't even let me take the money from the till. Finance company took my car. No money. No food in the house. I picked up this line of windshield stuff to sell. Six days. Seventy-five cents. Going crazy with worry. I saw that gun in a service station and stole it. No food in the house. No money for rent. Six days. . . ."

"Yes, yes, Jack," I interrupted—for he was becoming incoherent. He was cold and wet; probably hungry. I walked him across First Street to a restaurant.

We never did get that soup. Inside the restaurant, I went to a pay phone and called my city editor. He ordered me to rush over to the morgue and ride out with the "dead wagon" to pick up the body of a woman reported murdered.

Grabbing Bryan by the arm, I hurried him up an alley and into the morgue garage. Bill Corson, son of the City Coroner, was in the driver's seat. We piled in beside him and rolled out into the night.

Bryan didn't seem to know or to care what was happening. He sat there next to me, hunched and silent. I handed him two ten-dollar bills, but he pushed them aside, so I crumpled them and pushed them into the breast pocket of his coat.

Corson turned left beyond King Street station, and the wagon squished through mud and slush into Seattle's worst slum district—a section where poverty-stricken Italians lived in squalor. We pulled up before a ramshackle house over-flowing with wailing, moaning neighbors. Corson and I car-ried the basket, and Bryan followed.

We set the basket on the floor in a small bedroom in which the body of a large, work-worn woman lay on a broken-down bed. She hadn't been murdered—she'd dropped dead at her washtub.

Corson ushered the neighbors into the yard. The woman's husband and five small children remained at the foot of the bed, clutching cne another.

I'll never forget the misery in that husband's eyes. Bryan noticed it too, for as Corson and I lifted the heavy body into the basket, he walked to the man, and without a word, handed him one of the two ten-dollar bills I'd put in his pocket.

The husband sobbed, and the children began a sympathetic lament. Corson strapped down the lid, and we carried the basket through the mob of neighbors in the yard, and lifted it into the wagon.

As the three of us settled into the front seat, Bryan said,

"I've got to get home. Please—take me home. I must have been crazy. I didn't know what misery is."

Corson swung around to James Street and dropped Bryan and me off in front of a small white cottage. Bryan hurried up the steps. I followed, slowly. I paused in the little hall and watched through the kitchen door. With eyes closed, Bryan was holding his wife as if he'd never let her go. Two little girls, about three and five years old, were each hugging one of their daddy's legs.

Then Mrs. Bryan noticed me and moved out of her husband's arms. She came into the hall and shut the door. "He's been so worried and sick," she said, eyes filled with tears. "Tonight when he wasn't home by seven o'clock, I knelt down and prayed God to please take care of him, and to bring him home safely. And here he is."

I realized then, why the impulse to get to Pioneer Square had come to me at exactly seven. I felt awed and humble.

"His business went broke," Mrs. Bryan said, "but I'm not a bit worried. I've asked God to take care of that, too."

I looked into Mrs. Bryan's calm eyes and thought: It was this woman's faith in God that sent me out into this dismal night to bring her husband home to her.

I said, "I'm certain things will work out just as you want them to, Mrs. Bryan."

I told her to call me at the police station if she needed me, then stepped out onto the little porch. As the door closed behind me, I remembered that Bryan had given ten dollars to the Italian, so I turned back into the house. Father, mother, and the two little girls were kneeling at kitchen chairs, praying. I stood for a moment, then tiptoeing to the table put a few one-dollar bills on it and slipped out.

God did take care of Bryan's business. Today, automobile men up and down the Pacific Coast know him and his line of accessories.

Back at the police station press room, I picked up the phone and called the city desk. "That trip with Corson," I said.

"I'll give you a rewrite man," said the city editor.

"No—don't bother," I said. "There wasn't any story."

One of the greatest things about human beings is how they can and do so forget themselves when loving others that they will put their own lives on the line for them. And what is their reward? Not that they do what they do for reward. But there is a reward just the same, and it is joy. Beyond that, it is an inexpressible enthusiasm for life, for people and for God.

I would like to write *Finis* to this treasury of joy and enthusiasm with one of the most glorious statements ever made:

> But as it is written, Eye hath not seen, nor ear heard, neither have entered into the heart of man, the things which God hath prepared for them that love him.
>
> 1 Corinthians 2:9

Index of Authors and Titles

A Selected List of Cedar Books

While every effort is made to keep prices low, it is sometimes necessary to increase prices at short notice. Mandarin Paperbacks reserves the right to show new retail prices on covers which may differ from those previously advertised in the text or elsewhere.

The prices shown below were correct at the time of going to press.

All these books are available at your bookshop or newsagent, or can be ordered direct from the publisher. Just tick the titles you want and fill in the form below.

Mandarin Paperbacks, Cash Sales Department, PO Box 11, Falmouth, Cornwall TR10 9EN.

Please send cheque or postal order, no currency, for purchase price quoted and allow the following for postage and packing:

UK including BFPO — £1.00 for the first book, 50p for the second and 30p for each additional book ordered to a maximum charge of £3.00.

Overseas including Eire — £2 for the first book, £1.00 for the second and 50p for each additional book thereafter.

NAME (Block letters) ....

ADDRESS..

....

☐ I enclose my remittance for ....

☐ I wish to pay by Access/Visa Card Number ☐☐☐☐☐☐☐☐☐☐☐☐☐☐

Expiry Date ☐☐☐☐